Life *beneath* the
NORTHERN LIGHTS

edited by
Lizzy Pattison

uclan
University of Central Lancashire

uclanpublishing

UCLan Publishing is a not-for-profit trust specialising in publications and films which educate and inspire. All the work produced is undertaken by students at the University of Central Lancashire who work in partnership with local and global communities.

www.uclan.ac.uk

First edition

First published in 2014 by UCLan Publishing,
The University of Central Lancashire, ME316,
The Media Factory, Kirkham Street, Preston, PR1 2HE

British Library Cataloguing-in-Publication data
A catalogue record for this book is available from the British Library

ISBN 978-0-9565283-9-1

Designed, typeset and originated by Lizzy Pattison
Printed and bound in the UK by T. Snape & Co., Preston

CONTENTS

ACKNOWLEDGEMENTS

Many thanks to all the individuals who contributed to this book. Special thanks go to Alistair Hodge, Wayne Noble and Debbie Williams from UCLan Publishing for their support and advice; to Jonny Cooper from *Off the Map Travel* for his hard work to ensure that our research trip met, and exceeded, our expectations; to *Lights Over Lapland* photographer Chad Blakley for his expert advice and insight into aurora photography; and to *Naturum Abisko* for their information about the Sámi people.

Björkliden and Abisko

The research for this book was undertaken in Björkliden, an arctic haven 150 miles north of the Arctic Circle on the edge of the Abisko National Park – one of the last true wildernesses in Europe. Found on a hillside overlooking a vast arctic lake in northern Sweden and set among mighty mountains, this region is regarded as one of the best places to see the Northern Lights. Abisko is situated beneath the auroral oval, with dark skies and a weather shadow created by the surrounding peaks which cause more clear nights on average than other local destinations.

The Abisko National Park is a natural sanctuary that dominates the region. Established in 1909, the park covers 77 square kilometres (30 square miles) and is home to many species of birds and mammals including marten, stoat, the fell lemming, moose and reindeer, which are all common. Wolverines, arctic foxes, lynx and bears also inhabit the area but are only seen sporadically.

The creators of this book wish to thank the people of Björkliden and Abisko for their kind hospitality and for welcoming them so generously into their community.

PREFACE

This book provides an insight into how beliefs and perceptions about the Northern Lights have evolved over time. We look at early myths and legends belonging to cultures across the globe, at early scientific theory, and at what we now understand about the phenomenon. We also look closely at the culture of the Sámi people, indigenous to the Arctic, who lived beneath the Northern Lights and who were able to survive on one of the harshest terrains on Earth.

This book was initially inspired by reports that 2013 was to be the best year in a century to observe the Northern Lights. We researched the subject thoroughly from the UK, finding on the market no other book that combines the subjects outlined above, and then travelled over 2,000 miles to witness the phenomenon ourselves and to find out more about its history. It was here, in Abisko in Sweden, that we learned more about the Sámi people and the world-famous Ice Hotel, and were lucky enough to meet a number of people along the way who would go on to help us achieve our goal. The result is this informative and unique collaboration between our talented writers, illustrators and photographers.

Lizzy Pattison, December 2013

Photograph taken by Michael Jackson
in Abisko National Park, Sweden.

Photograph taken by Adam Shoker from the Aurora Sky
Station, overlooking Abisko National Park, Sweden.

1

WHAT IS THE AURORA?

The scientific explanation behind the mystical phenomenon

Adam Whittaker

The aurora polaris is a phenomenon that offers a unique experience to anyone who views it. It is made up of two auroral ovals: the aurora borealis, found at the North Pole, and the aurora australis, found at the South Pole. Appearing as a shimmering curtain of light in the night sky, it has amazed and astounded mankind for thousands of years. Understandably, many tales of the magical and supernatural have emerged over time, each attempting to explain the phenomenon, but only relatively recently have scientists found a demonstrable answer to this burning question. This answer has come about as a result of years of empirical study, scrupulous observations, and the meticulous gathering, recording, and analysis of data. An understanding of the aurora first requires an understanding of the Sun and of our planet, as well as some of the fundamentals of physics.

The Sun

At the centre of our solar system is the Sun: a huge ball of super-heated gas, or plasma, which accounts for over ninety-nine per cent of the total mass of the entire solar system. The gas in question is hydrogen, the lightest and most abundant element in the universe. Within every star, including our Sun, this gas is constantly undergoing nuclear fusion. This is a process whereby the hydrogen is converted into helium gas, the second most abundant and second lightest element in the universe, by means of a nuclear reaction which is responsible for the production of all the energy radiated by the Sun. It provides all of the light, heat, and energy necessary for life on Earth. Despite its relatively calm appearance when viewed from Earth with the naked eye, our star is an extremely complex, dynamic, and active

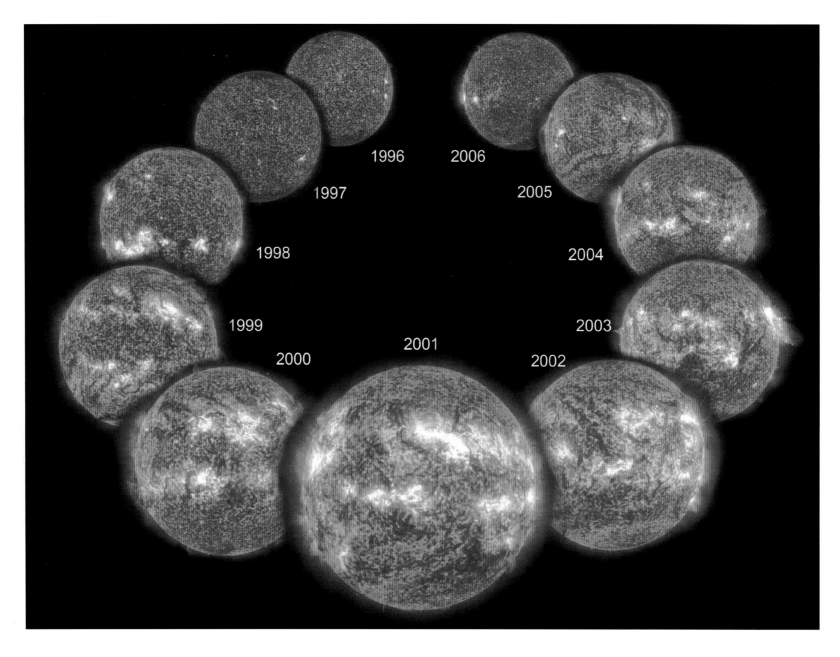

A section of the eleven-year cycle of the Sun, between 1996 and 2006. Image courtesy of SOHO (ESA and NASA).

object, and it is this activity that causes the Northern Lights, the 'aurora borealis'.

The Sun has an eleven-year cycle of activity, which peaks and troughs regularly, and which is responsible for what is known as space weather. At the beginning of the cycle, activity on the Sun is high, a state known as solar maximum; this takes approximately five and a half years to peak. After this, activity on the Sun decreases, to solar minimum, reaching the trough where activity is at its lowest point after another five and a half years, before it returns, once again, to the beginning of the cycle, and solar maximum. At its minimum level of activity the Sun is still dynamic, but, in comparison to solar maximum, this is considered to be calm space weather. Even at its lowest point, the activity exhibited by the Sun is far greater than anything encountered on Earth, so while terms such as solar minimum and solar maximum are frequently used to describe the Sun, it is important to remember that this is an active body which undergoes far more extreme climate conditions than Earth.

The activity associated with the solar cycle manifests itself in several ways. Observations of the Sun have revealed three of the principal types of activity to be sunspots, solar flares, and coronal mass ejections. Sunspots are dark spots on the photosphere, the outer shell of the Sun from which light radiates, which are cooler than the surrounding area and therefore appear darker in colour. These are temporary

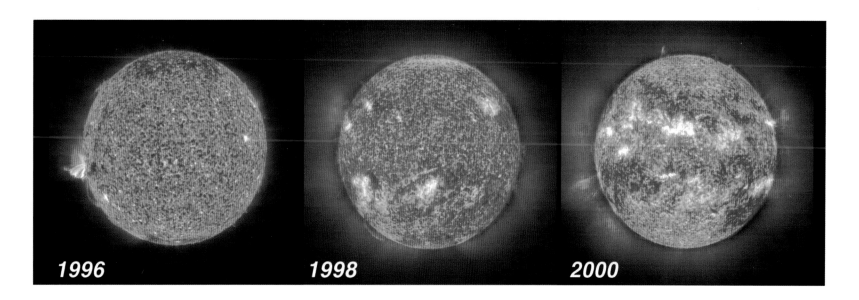

Three images of the Sun showing increasing sunspot activity. Image courtesy of SOHO (ESA and NASA).

phenomena which are caused by intense magnetic activity, and generally appear in pairs. Solar flares occur when plasma erupts and is flung upwards, after which it then rains back down onto the Sun. A coronal mass ejection (CME) is very similar to a solar flare, and occurs when the erupting plasma has enough energy to break free from the Sun and travel into space. These ejections are incredibly energetic and travel at a very rapid rate, which is necessary for the material to

overcome the gravitational pull of the Sun and achieve what is known as escape velocity. This is the speed at which an object or objects must travel in order to escape permanently the gravity of another object in space. This speed is variable and it is calculated based upon the mass of the object that is to be escaped from. The more massive the object is, the greater its gravitational pull and thus its escape velocity. CMEs are also very dangerous if they interact with humans in space. For example, if a CME had occurred when the Apollo astronauts were on the Moon, there would have been no way for them to escape to the safety of Earth in time to avoid it.

In addition to these phenomena, the Sun also produces 'solar wind'. This is not wind as we understand it on Earth, generated by the flow of warm and cold air around the planet. The solar wind is a stellar wind, produced by stars, and it consists of charged particles which stream outwards from the Sun in every direction, travelling at approximately one million miles per hour. All stars produce wind of this type and they do so to varying degrees of intensity.

The heliosphere is a huge 'bubble' that is 'blown' by the Sun by means of the solar wind, and it is within this bubble that the solar system resides. The farther from the Sun the solar wind travels, the weaker the influence of the Sun becomes, and eventually it approaches a boundary known as the termination shock. This is the point at which the particles of the solar wind are travelling at subsonic speeds, or slower than

A coronal mass ejection (CME).
Image courtesy of SOHO (ESA and NASA).

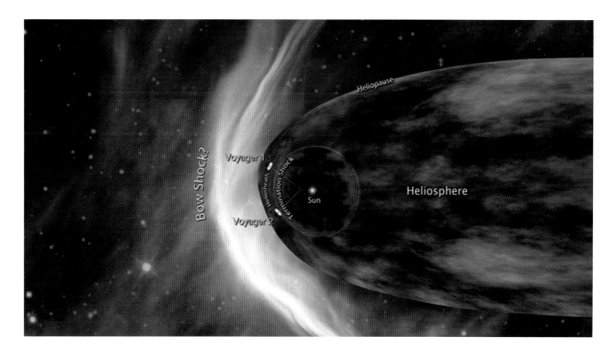

A diagram of the heliopause. Image courtesy of the NASA JPL and Caltech.

the speed of sound. There is a second, more distant boundary known as the heliopause. The heliopause is the point at which the pressure of the solar wind pushing outward from the Sun is equal to the pressure exerted by the interstellar medium, that is the material in space between the stars, and the stellar winds produced by other stars close by. This is the edge of the bubble. The area between the termination shock and the heliopause is known as the heliosheath. Because the Sun is travelling through space, taking with it the solar system, a wave forms in front of it as it travels, and this is called the bow shock. This can be visualised by imagining a boat travelling through water. As it does so it creates a wave that goes before it. In recent years NASA has collected new data which contradict this theory, suggesting that there may be no bow shock at all. The heliosphere is so large that the Voyager probes which were launched by NASA in the 1970s are now, some four decades later and counting, only just beginning to reach the threshold between the heliosphere and interstellar space, or the space between the stars. NASA is attempting to explore this region with the Interstellar Boundary Explorer mission, or IBEX, which will examine how the solar wind interacts with the interstellar medium.

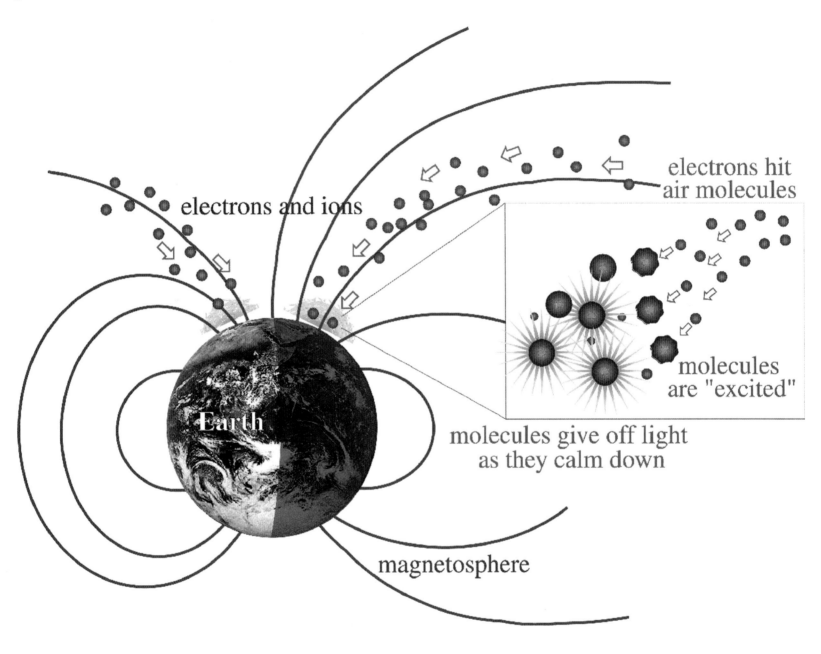

Earth's magnetic poles. Image courtesy of NASA.

CMEs, solar flares and the solar wind are the causes of the aurora, and the significance of a solar maximum is that it causes more and greater interactions between Earth and the Sun, and therefore auroras (or 'aurorae') which are viewed during a solar maximum are usually more spectacular, energetic and, ultimately, more beautiful.

Earth

The interaction between the Earth and the Sun is responsible for the aurora borealis. Earth generates an invisible magnetic bubble, or magnetic field, called the magnetosphere. This magnetic bubble encloses the planet in a protective shield, preventing us from being subjected to an array of toxic sources, such as radiation from the Sun or from other sources, such as cosmic rays. The Sun produces vast amounts of radiation which is hazardous to life, in particular ultra-violet light, although some of this does manage to get through the magnetosphere: if you are exposed to it you will, depending upon your skin complexion, receive either a sun tan or sun burn. The magnetosphere is generated deep inside Earth, in the core of the planet. Composed mostly of nickel and iron, the core has two separate and distinct parts. The inner core is solid and the outer core is molten, and therefore very hot. The rotation of the Earth has the effect of producing convection currents in this molten metal. Convection is the transfer of heat within a material where the material itself does not move as a whole; thus, the heat

in the hotter parts of the liquid metal core is moving to the cooler areas, and the currents produced by this transfer of heat generate the magnetic field of the magnetosphere. This is sometimes referred to as the Dynamo Effect. The magnetosphere is active and energetic. Magnetite deposits on Earth show us that it 'flips' every so often, so that the poles change over, reversing the polarity of the magnetosphere. The next time the polarity flips it will cause compasses to point south rather than north.

The magnetosphere is an invisible magnetic field that emanates from the poles. This is not true of all planets. Mars, for example, has lost almost all of its magnetic field over time because its core has solidified, making it not only an aurora-free world, but also causing the surface of the red planet to be much more susceptible to the ravages of solar and cosmic radiation. Contrastingly, Jupiter, the largest planet in the solar system, generates a huge magnetic field. This is far greater in strength and intensity than Earth's magnetic field, and would be extremely toxic to humans due to its ability to generate powerful radiation belts by trapping and accelerating radioactive particles. The core of Jupiter is made of hydrogen, which ordinarily is not able to produce electricity or magnetism. In this case, however, the enormous weight of Jupiter's upper atmosphere subjects the hydrogen in the core to pressure equivalent to millions of times that of the atmospheric pressure on Earth, and under these conditions hydrogen is thought to enter an exotic state and become metallic, and is subsequently able to conduct electricity. This process is thought to account for the magnetic field that is generated around Jupiter. Given the variations we observe in our own solar system alone, it is clear that we reside in a sort of magnetic oasis, a 'sweet spot' where the conditions are safe enough to protect us from the harmful radiation produced by our star, but also interesting and energetic enough to allow us to observe one of the great wonders of the world, the Northern Lights.

Sun–Earth interaction

The interaction between the Earth's magnetism and electrically charged particles from the Sun is what creates the aurora borealis. The charged particles of the solar wind, electrons, stream towards Earth and collide with the gases in the Earth's atmosphere, made up mainly of nitrogen and oxygen. In the process of colliding, the electrons deliver energy to the magnetosphere and the energy is temporarily stored there as electrical currents and electromagnetic energy. This is not a stable state for the magnetosphere, however, and the energy is prone to sudden release. When this happens the energy accelerates electrons in the magnetosphere and they are funnelled down towards the poles where they collide with gas atoms in the atmosphere. This in turn excites the atoms, causing them to become more energetic. The atoms of gas in the atmosphere consist of an atomic nucleus, the centre of an atom, and a cloud of electrons which orbit the nucleus. In order for an atom to become excited the electrons must be pushed farther away from the nucleus. This is a higher energy orbit. The atoms do not retain this energy indefinitely and remain this way, however, and so they must undergo the process of returning to their previous state and

Jupiter's auroras. Image courtesy of NASA.

that means that the electrons return to a lower energy orbit, closer to the nucleus. The energy that the atoms gain from the solar wind must go somewhere, for energy cannot be destroyed or simply disappear; it can only be converted into other forms of energy. It must obey the laws of physics. In the case of the aurora borealis the energy is released again, this time in the form of photons, or light. It is this light that we see shimmering in the skies as the aurora borealis. The more energetic the Sun, the more energy is delivered to, and subsequently released by, the atoms in the atmosphere, and the more light is produced. The more light that is produced, the more spectacular the aurora that is observed.

Auroras occur at the Earth's magnetic poles and are named aurora borealis and aurora australis for the north and south poles respectively. When viewed from space, as they often are by astronauts on board the International Space Station, auroras are visible as doughnut-shaped rings above the poles. These are known as the auroral ovals (see the diagram on page 24). In the past auroras of varying strength have been observed at locations on Earth that are some distance from the poles. This is rare, and only happens during periods of intense solar activity. While it is not unheard of to observe auroras as far down the globe from the poles as mainland Europe, due to the rarity of the conditions required for this to happen it is unlikely. For those wishing to observe the aurora polaris the polar regions offer by far the best opportunity to do so. Auroras

must be observed at night, because however spectacular or breathtaking they appear, they cannot compete with the copious amount of light delivered to Earth during the day by the Sun.

The human eye has evolved to be receptive to just a small proportion of the light (known as the visible spectrum) which exists in the universe. White light that we see is an amalgamation of the seven colours of the rainbow and the retina does not split light into the rainbow. We need nature to do the for us by a process known as refraction, and it usually occurs when the light passes through raindrops, hence a rainbow is observed. Each of us is accustomed to seeing light as white light and each of us is used to the change observed when going from dark to light environments, or vice versa. The pupil is the aperture through which light enters the eye, expanding in the dark to allow more light in, and contracting to prevent too much light entering the eye in bright ambient conditions. As a consequence any white light that enters the eye will inhibit observations of an aurora, because the pupil will contract, thus allowing less light to hit the retina. This means that less light from the aurora will enter the eye. It can take around thirty minutes for the eye to adapt fully to the dark, and so observing the aurora must be done in as dark an area as possible, not only to keep the eye adapted, but also the darker the background, the greater the contrast between it and an aurora, and thus the sharper the image will be. Fortunately, it is possible to use a torch to find one's way around in the dark while aurora-hunting. Red light does not affect the retina in the same way as other colours, allowing the retina to remain adapted to dark conditions, and so it is vital to carry a red torch as standard to get the best views possible. This applies to all night-time observational astronomy. It is also vital to avoid general light pollution caused by buildings, street lighting and other man-made infrastructure.

It is not unusual to observe auroras in many different shapes over the course of a single night, and this is something that has yet to be understood fully and properly. An aurora can shimmer, curtain-like, across the sky, or appear in spirals, waves, or bands. Each aurora is unique, and will constantly shift and change for the duration of its appearance.

Typically auroras are observed in several different colours. By far the most commonly observed is green, with red, blue, pink, white, and purple appearing rarely. Different coloured auroras are observed because of the different gases that are producing them. Green auroras are produced by oxygen at lower altitudes. Oxygen at higher altitudes typically produces red, while nitrogen produces blue, often observed as purple due to atmospheric conditions and other light mixing. This mixing of light from auroras can also produce pink or white auroras. Observing red auroras is much more challenging. If one visualises a household curtain as an aurora, then

Venus, Jupiter and the aurora borealis. Photograph taken by *Lights Over Lapland* photographer Chad Blakley. Exposure: 6.0 sec; f/2.8; ISO 1600.

the bottom of the curtain is the green aurora, and the top of the curtain is the red aurora. When standing directly underneath the curtain it will be impossible to see the red section as it is obscured by the green. Red auroras are more easily observed at lower latitudes, the consequence of which is that they are harder to observe than at the poles.

The production of different colours in this way is similar to what is commonly referred to as neon lighting. Under standard conditions neon is an inert, or 'noble', gas (one of six such gases, the others being argon, helium, krypton, radon and xenon). Inert means that such elements possess a low degree of chemical reactivity, and so inert gases will rarely combine with other elements to form compounds. For example, you will almost certainly never have heard of helium dioxide because that would be a compound of helium and oxygen. Each of the noble gases glows when an electrical current is passed through it, differing from other methods such as illumination using halogens which produce a full spectrum of light when they glow, including light not visible to humans such as ultraviolet. While the everyday term for light generated using electricity and noble gas is 'neon' lighting, each gas produces a different colour, so the term is something of a misnomer, since neon is one of the six gases which can produce light in this way. Just as the noble gases glow in different colours, so the atmospheric gases on Earth produce different coloured auroras, albeit via a different process.

In the past there have been claims of sounds emitted by auroras, with reports of hissing, crackling and fizzing noises. Sound is a compression wave which is conducted through oxygen. At auroral altitudes the air is too thin to conduct sound, and none has yet been detected by scientists. It is possible that the reports of sounds are actually coming from static electricity crackling in the observer's hair.

Auroras and solar exploration

The Sun is explored continuously using space-borne probes or satellites and, as time has passed, the technology used to observe it has become more and more sophisticated. Early discoveries concerning the solar wind and causes of the aurora borealis came from the early space programme, with one notable discovery being the existence of coronal holes. These are areas of the Sun where the plasma in the corona, the part of the Sun that can be thought of as the atmosphere of the star, is less dense and cooler than the rest. This discovery came about as a result of X-ray observations made by the NASA Skylab mission, launched and completed in the 1970s following the Apollo moon landings. When a coronal hole faces Earth the result is an increase in the influence and in the various effects of the solar wind.

The now-completed THEMIS (Time History of Events and Macroscale Interactions during Substorms) mission launched by NASA in 2007 was sent to determine the cause of extremely dynamic auroras. This was a constellation of five satellites that were tasked with understanding the energetic auroras capable of endangering astronauts and damaging telecommunications satellites orbiting Earth. THEMIS specifically studied substorms, events where the magneto-sphere is bombarded so heavily by the solar wind that it causes disruptions in power lines, often damaging electrical equipment. Upon completion of this mission the satellites were still operational, and so were re-tasked to study other phenomena.

SOHO (Solar Heliospheric Observatory) is an ongoing mission which, since its launch in 1995, has studied the Sun in great detail, attempting to understand the dynamics of the star and how the way the Sun works affects the way in which it interacts with the rest of the solar system. One of the most recent missions to explore the Sun is the Solar Dynamics Observatory, or SDO. The SDO is currently imaging the Sun in greater detail than ever before, using its extremely powerful CCD (charge-coupled device) imaging sensor. This type of sensor is now commonly found in modern mobile phones and is regarded as one of the most significant advances in imaging technology, allowing the gathering and processing of light in much more sophisticated ways than ever before. This technology has enabled imaging in many fields of astronomy to improve dramatically. The images returned by the SDO are of a higher resolution than anything seen before, and this is important because the greater the resolution, the finer the detail we are able to see. The SDO is capable of imaging solar flares and CMEs, and NASA regularly publishes such images and animations of these phenomena. This is the current state of solar exploration; we are able to watch eruptions and ejections taking place on our star, which are extraordinarily energetic and powerful, and we may do so safely at home from a computer screen. Even more remarkable than that, the NASA website provides a live feed of the Sun, displaying an image of the Sun as it is at any given moment, using the cameras on board the SDO. Now THAT is reality television!

The exploration of the Sun has slowly built up an astonishingly rich and detailed understanding of not only its workings, but also its interactions with Earth, of which auroras are the most beautiful, wondrous and awe inspiring. Despite the rich array of mythologies and stories that has developed over the centuries, the scientific understanding of the aurora is equally, if not more, fascinating. Since the dawn of the space age study of the Sun has slowly pieced together the knowledge that now explains the aurora borealis and the processes behind it. Human knowledge has expanded from a simple understanding of the weather cycles to a more detailed and scientific comprehension of the way in which auroras are formed. It is now believed that the phenomenon is caused by a star slamming pieces of itself into the magnetosphere of a planet which is itself a product of processes occurring deep inside a cooling rock is racing around a star year after year. This interaction is seen on Earth as the Northern Lights.

Photograph taken by Adam Shoker in Björkliden, Sweden.

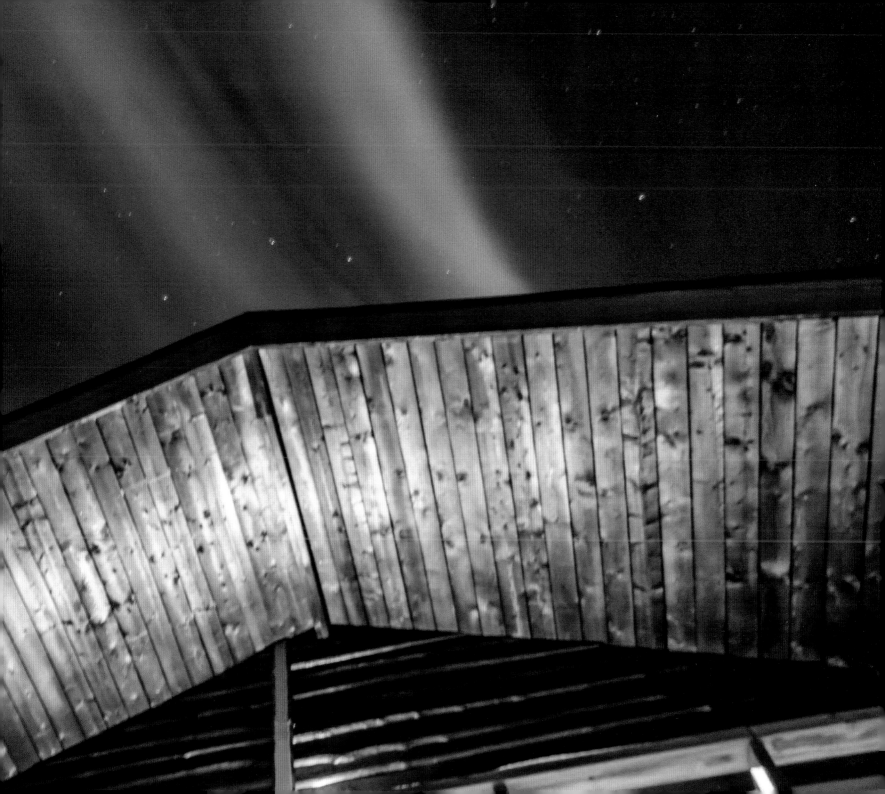

Photograph taken by *Lights Over Lapland* photographer Chad Blakley. Exposure: 6.4 sec; f/3.5; ISO 1600.

2

THE NORTHERN LIGHTS THROUGH HISTORY

A journey to understanding, from myth to fact

Claire Edmonds

Beliefs about the aurora borealis have altered and evolved, constantly, throughout history. The first written record of the aurora dates back to 2600 BC, in China: 'Fu-Pao, the mother of the Yellow Empire Shuan-Yuan, saw strong lightning moving around the star Su, which belongs to the constellation of Bei-Dou, and the light illuminated the whole area.' There is also a Cro-Magnon cave painting from southern France, dating back to around 30,000 BC, which is believed to depict the aurora, and, if it does, is the earliest surviving record of the phenomenon.

There are believed to be several references to the aurora in the Old Testament of the Bible. For example, *Ezekiel*, Chapter 1, Verse 4, reads: 'And I looked, and, behold, a whirlwind came out of the north, a great cloud, and a fire infolding itself, and a brightness was about it, and out of the midst thereof as the colour of amber, out of the midst of the sky.'

The phenomenon was also present in ancient Greek and Roman literature. Plutarch in 467 BC wrote that, 'During seventy days there was an enormous and furious figure in the sky. It was like a flaming cloud, which did not stay at its position but moved windingly and regularly, so that the glowing fragments were flying in all directions and fire was blazing as the comets do.' This is, however, widely believed to be a reference to an earlier record of the event written by Anaxagoras.

There were even some attempts by ancient Greek thinkers to explain the aurora. For example, in 593 BC Hippocrates and Aeschylus developed the theory that the aurora was caused by sunlight reflecting off of the surface of the Earth.

Later, in 350 BC, in *Meteorology* Aristotle recorded his belief that the aurora was caused by steam rising from the surface of the Earth, encountering the light from the Sun, and burning, producing wonderful colours.

For many hundreds of years after these early recorded sightings, spectacular displays of glowing, dancing waves against dark night skies were regarded with awe. Their presence influenced folklore and religion, and provided an intellectual challenge for scientists determined to find their cause.

Cro-Magnon cave painting 'macronis' believed to depict the aurora borealis. Courtesy of THEMIS consortium. THEMIS is a project of international cooperation between NASA, JPL-Caltech and Arizona State University.

Bust of Plutarch,
Museum of the Temple of Delphi.

Bust of Hippocrates,
British Museum.

Bust of Aeschylus,
Museum of Capitoline, Rome.

Bust of Aristotle,
Roman copy of Greek original.

Before the Age of Enlightenment the aurora caused as much mystification as fascination. With no widely accepted scientific explanation for the lights, many different mythical beliefs formed. These were passed down through cultures and found their way into works of literature and art.

During the Middle Ages, the majority of the beliefs about the aurora reflected the superstitious nature of the people. It was common for the link to be made between the lights and religion, and many European cultures believed the lights to be a message from their maker signalling impending war, disease or death. At this latitude the aurora would appear as red in colour, which may have further influenced their negative associations with the phenomenon.

In the *Konungs Skuggsjá* (or 'King's Mirror'), a Norse book written in the thirteenth century, further attempts were made to give a scientific explanation to the aurora. The first theory relies on the medieval idea that the world was flat and surrounded by sea; the phenomenon was caused by the light from fires surrounding the oceans, only visible in a clear, dark sky. The second theory was that the light came from the Sun's beams reflected up into the sky from its position below the horizon. The third theory was that glaciers could absorb power, and once they had absorbed enough power they would radiate flames, which would reflect light up into the sky.

As science moved forward, the way the aurora borealis was explained started to evolve. Until the early twentieth

A red and green aurora. Photograph taken by *Lights Over Lapland*. Photographer Chad Blakley. Exposure 8.9 sec; f/2.8; ISO 1600.

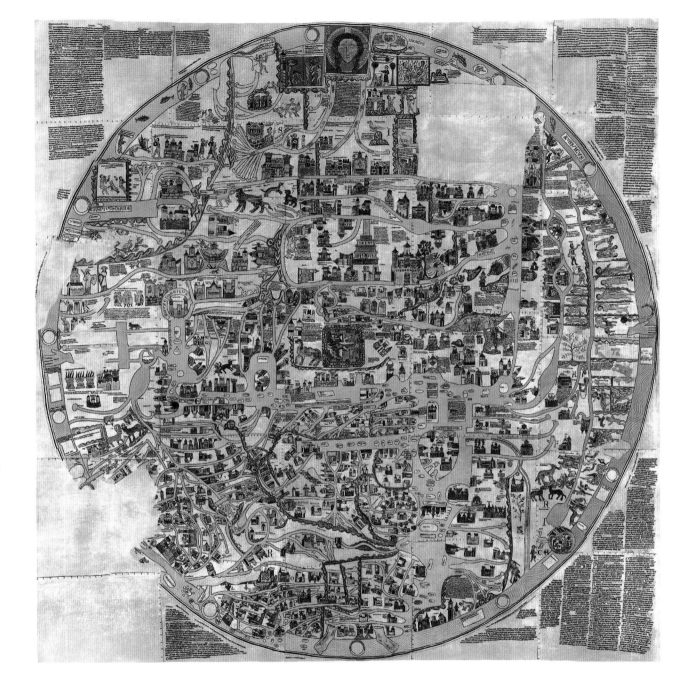

The Ebstorf Map, originally attributed to Gervase of Ebstorf monastery. Historians have estimated that the map was created between 1234 and 1300. It was discovered in a German monastery in 1843, measures 12ft × 12ft, and is made of 30 goatskins stitched together. The map depicts medieval European beliefs about how the world might look. Notably, they believed the world was round, but flat; disk shaped, rather than globe shaped.

century the study of the aurora was limited to observation, and many scientists sought to solve the mystery of their origin. As the field of science developed, so did the understanding that everything we can see has a cause. This meant that scientific explanations slowly started to replace the centuries-old superstitions, myths and legends.

In the seventeenth century the Northern Lights were given their scientific name, aurora borealis, but there is some dispute as to who should be credited for this. Some believe it was Galileo Galilei in 1616, while others believe it was a French mathematician, Gassend, in 1649. The naming of the phenomenon coincided with the beginning of the Maunder Minimum, a period where the aurora is absent from records for approximately a century, and when Spörer, a German astronomer, recorded only 50 sunspots during a 30-year period of observation, compared with an average of 40,000–50,000 over the same length of time now.

The next occurrence of the aurora would not be until 1716, when Sir Edmund Halley (of Halley's Comet) offered a theory about the aurora in his paper *An Account of the Late Surprizing Appearance of the Lights Seen in the Air, on the Sixth of March Last; With an Attempt to Explain the*

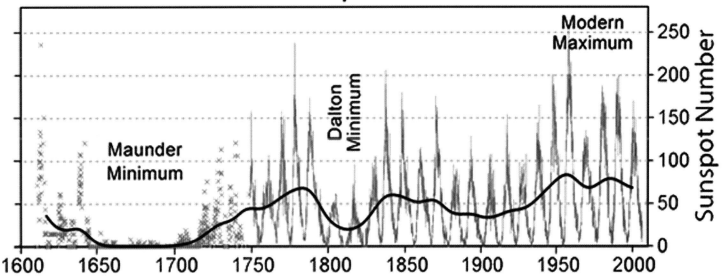

A diagram showing recorded sunspot activity between approximately 1600 and 2000.

Principal Phaenomena thereof. He observed the position of the lights in the sky as being 'low under the Pole and very near due North', and speculated that 'our globe of Earth is no other than one great magnet'. He suggested that 'lum'nous vapour' might be drawn towards the two magnetic poles, in the north and the south, as metal dust on a surface is drawn towards the two poles of a magnet.

Benjamin Franklin, sixth President of Pennsylvania and a scientist famous for his experiments involving electricity, witnessed the aurora during an Atlantic crossing in the late 1700s. His theory, following this experience, was that the Lights were caused by a high concentration of electrical charges in the extreme, polar, regions, the inevitable release of which caused the visible light display.

Following this, in 1790, a British natural philosopher and scientist called Henry Cavendish developed a new observation technique for the aurora. Using this he was able to estimate that the light emitted during the auroral display is created at an altitude of around 100–130km, or approximately 60 miles above the surface of the Earth.

In the nineteenth century there was a renewed effort to understand the aurora borealis. Expeditions were launched,

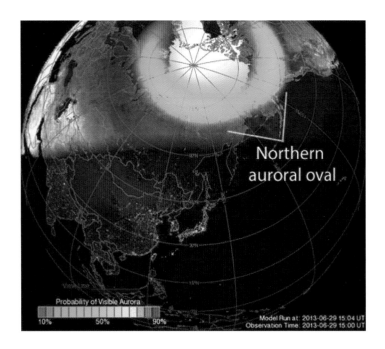
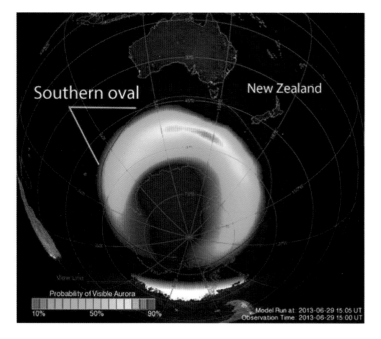

The northern and southern auroral ovals, 29 June 2013.
Image courtesy of NOAA.

and a number of key observations were made, and proved. For example, in 1868, a Swedish physicist called Anders Jonas Ångström proved that auroral light differs from sunlight. This revealed that the phenomenon could not be caused by any kind of reflection, and might, therefore, be caused by a gas in the atmosphere. In 1883 Sophus Tromholt, a Danish astrophysicist, organised a network of observation stations for the purpose of collecting data about the aurora. He was the first to observe the auroral oval, and successfully demonstrated the correlation between the appearance of the aurora and the 11-year sunspot cycle.

The real breakthrough came in 1902, when a Norwegian physicist called Kristian Birkeland, who had turned his attention to the aurora several years previously, made a significant discovery. By using specially designed experiments he deduced that the light we can see is caused by currents flowing through the gas of the upper atmosphere. This strengthened the theory put forward by Franklin back in the 1700s, and suggested that the phenomenon did indeed involve electricity.

Birkeland dedicated himself to a series of experiments which worked on the premise that electrons came from the Sun, and were guided to the polar regions of Earth by our magnetic field. As part of his research Birkeland led a number of expeditions into the very north of Norway, and it was here that he became the first to compile accounts and data from multiple sightings of the aurora. He collected magnetic field data, and with this he was able to chart the pattern of the electric currents. He developed a theory which suggested that electrons, directed at Earth, were ejected from the surface of the Sun. These electrons were then guided to the polar regions of Earth by our geomagnetic field. In doing this, they interacted with the specific atmosphere of the Earth, and this is what produces the visible aurora. This is the basis of current scientific understanding of the aurora. It later became a widely respected theory, despite being ridiculed by Birkeland's fellow scientists at the time.

Definitive proof that Birkeland's theory was right was finally produced in 1967. A probe had been sent into space, which allowed observation of the magnetic disturbances passing over the polar regions. Sadly, Birkeland did not live to see his life's work accepted as fact.

The aurora borealis remains a source of wonder for those who see it, and is explored to this day by scientists striving for a better understanding of the phenomenon. However, many myths about the magical lights remain, woven deeply into the cultures that held them, and serve to provide a fascinating insight into our past.

Above
Dr Kristian Birkeland, 1900.

Photograph taken by Adam Shoker.
from Abisko National Park, Sweden.

'AURORA BOREALIS'

Perhaps the most enduring myth about the aurora borealis comes from ancient Greece. It tells the story of the goddess of the dawn, Aurora, and her son, Boreas.

Claire Edmonds

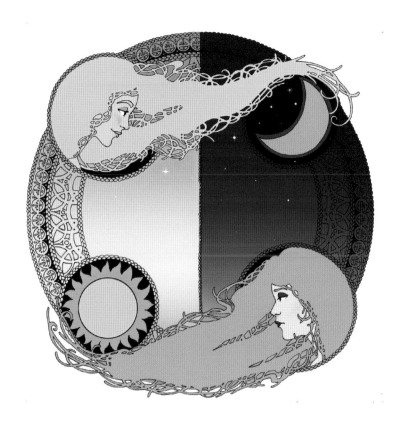

Aurora, or Eos as she was known in Greek mythology, was the sister of Helios (the Sun) and Selene (the Moon). Eos was believed to wake before anything or anyone else. The Northern Lights were said to be very bright, almost like a night-time dawn, and were believed to be caused by Aurora riding her mighty chariot across the sky to announce the arrival of Helios, opening the gates of heaven to bring in each new day. Boreas, one of the four winds, was believed to cause the wind that makes the Northern Lights dance.

According to the myth, the duties of Eos do not end there. When Helios (the Sun) arrives, she transforms into Hemera (the Day) and acts as a companion for him. As time passes, she transforms once more, into Hespera (the Dusk) until it is time to bid goodbye to Helios, and join Selene (the Moon). The cycle is completed when it is time to renew herself into Aurora once more, to welcome the dawn.

Illustration by Wensdi Dougherty.

Photograph taken by *Lights Over Lapland*
photographer Chad Blakley. 1.6 sec; f/1.4; ISO 1600.

4

AURORA MYTHOLOGY

From dragons to dancers, foxes to spirits ... the myths surrounding the aurora borealis are almost as spectacular as the lights themselves

Dee Devine. Illustrated by Broady Blackwell

Sápmi

The Sámi people traditionally lived in a vast Arctic area called Sápmi which encompasses parts of northern Finland, Norway, Russia and Sweden. These indigenous people have an unparalleled proximity to the Northern Lights, and a number of legends to explain the phenomenon have formed over time.

One long-standing belief was that people should behave solemnly and respectfully whenever the lights were in the sky. This was because the lights were thought to comprise the energies of the souls of the dead, which meant that bad fortune awaited anyone who showed them disrespect. Because of this many people chose to keep their families indoors when the lights were on display. If you did find yourself outside it was probably best not to whistle a tune, because the Sámi people believed that whistling under the lights would summon them closer and closer, until they whisked you away!

Sámi beliefs about the Northern Lights were not all negative, however. The lights were also considered to have the power to aid conflict resolution.

China and Japan

In China, the lights were believed to be the fiery breath of dragons fighting in the sky! Some even think that the Chinese began using the image of dragons after watching the lights, with the auroral swirls providing inspiration for the curved shapes of the popular Chinese symbol.

The Chinese also linked the lights to fertility and childbirth. It is still believed in both Chinese and Japanese cultures that a child conceived under the Northern Lights will be blessed with good fortune for the duration of his or her life.

Scotland

In Scotland, the Lights are called *Fir Chlis* meaning 'the merry dancers' or 'the nimble men' in Scottish Gaelic. This is due to their graceful movements. Another Scottish belief was that the lights were actually clans at war and that blood spilled in violent battle was the true cause of the red lights.

United States of America

The Fox Indians of Wisconsin saw the Northern Lights as an ill omen. They feared the lights, believing that they were the ghosts of slain enemies waiting to take deadly revenge.

The Makah Indians believed the Lights were caused by dwarfs lighting bright colourful fires. Meanwhile the Mandan Indians believed the lights were fires upon which soldiers from the northern lands were slowly cooking their dead enemies in huge pots.

The Algonquian Indians did not have such a negative view of the lights – they believed that after Nanahbozho created the Earth, he travelled to the far north where he builds great fires, the light from which reflects southward to remind people of his everlasting love.

Greenland

One of the names for Northern Lights in Greenland is *alugsukat*, which means 'secret birth'. This is because according to folklore of the Eskimos of eastern Greenland, the lights are considered to be the souls of stillborn babies.

Scandinavia

The Scandinavian name for the aurora translates as 'herring flash'. This is because it was believed that the dancing whirls of green light were a reflection of huge shoals of herring in the sea, and whenever the Lights were visible, fishermen were expected to be blessed with good catches of fish.

According to Swedish legend, a winter with frequent displays of the Northern Lights served to predict a good yield of crops the following year.

In Norwegian folklore, the Northern Lights were thought to be the spirits of old maids dancing in the sky and waving at those below them.

According to one popular Finnish myth, magical arctic foxes sweeping their tails across the snow and spraying it into the sky is the real reason for the spectacular light show. In fact, the Finnish name for the Northern Lights even translates as 'fox fires'.

Norse mythology connected the aurora borealis with war. It was believed that the lights appeared when sunlight reflected on the shiny shields of the Valkyries who were racing across the sky on the way to their resting place,

Valhalla. In old Icelandic folklore, it was believed that the Northern Lights would ease the pain of childbirth. It was not all good news for mothers though – it was also thought that pregnant women looking at the lights would give birth to cross-eyed children.

Canada

The Eskimos of Labrador in north-east Canada believed the Northern Lights to be torches lit by the dead who were playing soccer in the heavens with a walrus skull. Indeed, the Eskimo word for the Northern Lights is *aksarnirq*, which translates literally as 'ball player'.

In north-west Canada, meanwhile, the Eskimos of the lower Yukon River believed the lights were the beautiful dances of animal spirits.

The Eskimos of Hudson Bay also associated the Lights with bad omens, believing that they were caused by spilled light from the lanterns of demons searching for tragic lost souls.

Estonia

In Estonian mythology, the Northern Lights are said to occur when a celestial war or wedding is taking place. The Lights are the reflections of the sleighs and horses drawing the parties.

Another Estonian legend connects the aurora to whales playing in the sky.

Photograph taken by Adam
Shoker in Björkliden, Sweden.

5

'FOX FIRES'

Finnish people traditionally believed that the Lights were caused by a magical fox sweeping his tail as he ran across the snow, spraying crystals high into the sky. Their name for this phenomenon, *'revontulet'*, translates as 'fox fires'.

Claire Edmonds. Illustrated by Amy Freeman

The sled made an unmistakeable crunching sound as it glided over the packed white crystals below. Hannu tightened his grip on the leather reins as he guided his dogs along the track they knew so well. His four passengers were snug and content, wrapped up warm against the bracing wind. Hannu was happy; he never felt so alive as when he was out in the dark night, under the light-pricked sky. It was just a shame that the beautiful aurora borealis was not out to play this evening.

It was a particularly clear night, with each star clearly defined above. They were making good progress and would reach their destination ahead of time. The dogs ran on, enjoying the run as much as Hannu, their paws sure in the thick snow, the sound of their panting punctuating the air.

The frozen lake, so serene and rippled in the summer, was a place Hannu particularly loved to be. A wide expanse of flat ice framed with snow dipped trees, which twinkled in the starlight as though freshly dusted with glitter. Going past the lake would have been a more direct route for them this evening, but he could not pass up the opportunity to glide across this serene spot.

He was not the only one to have that idea. Ahead of them, a snowy arctic fox ran deftly across the ice. Instinctively Hannu slowed the dogs, not wanting to scare the creature and dissuade it from its purpose.

The fox was undeterred by having an audience and ran on, only slowing when it seemed to change its mind mid-route. As it spun to change direction, its bushy broom-like tail swept across the ice, disturbing the delicate sparkling powder which lay on top of it, sending it flying into the air.

Spray would be expected, but it did not stop. The snowflakes floated in slow motion, seeming to take on a life of their own as they drifted ever higher. Then something truly magical happened – something which Hannu had heard talk of, but in his years living below the Northern Lights, had never believed to be true.

He watched in amazement and wonder as the white icy crystals reached high above and turned the sky pretty shades of green. A shimmering, dancing curtain of perfect ethereal light. Hannu and his passengers gasped in awe at what they had witnessed, small murmurs of conversations passing between them as they tried to make sense of something which, in terms of logic, could not be explained.

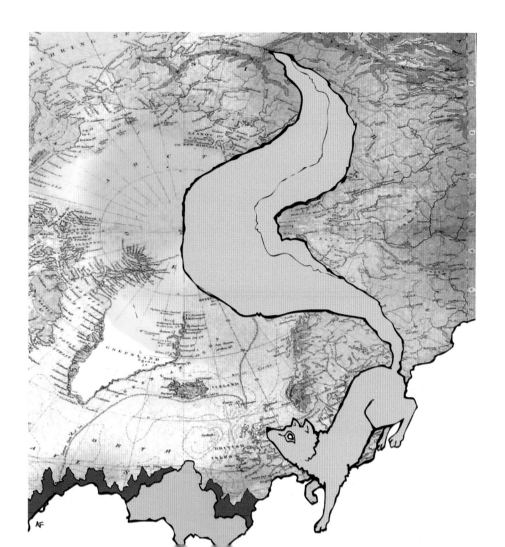

Photograph taken by Adam Shoker from the
Aurora Sky Station, Abisko National Park, Sweden.

6

DANCE OF THE SPIRITS

Traditionally, Cree people believed in a 'circle of life', where each individual's essence is found in their spirit. Death does not sever ties to loved ones because the spirits of the deceased find alternative ways to communicate with them. Part of this belief involved the aurora borealis, which was perceived as spirits of the departed dancing for their loved ones who were still on the mortal plane.

Claire Edmonds. Illustrated by Ciaran Collins

Standing in the rain, Kimmie wasn't sure where her tears ended and the water falling from the skies began. In just two short weeks the colours in her world had dulled and there was an ache in her heart which felt as if it would never leave. An endless carousel of well-meaning friends had constantly circled her, a babble of suffocating kindness, when all she had wanted was to be alone. Because she was alone. The home she had once loved was now nothing but a shell with empty beds and chairs, the imprints of bodies still in their soft seats. It hadn't been like this when her dad had died. She hadn't really known him. He'd left before she'd learned to ride a bike or had her first crush and when he tried to mend their tattered relationship years later, it had

been too late. Kimmie had barely noticed the disappearance of birthday cards with money tucked inside and the glitter-covered Christmas cards.

This was different. Her mum was all she'd had; they had been a team. It was her who had placed money under the pillow in exchange for a bloodied tooth while her gap-smiled daughter pretended to sleep, who took her to buy her first bra and then padded out her underdeveloped chest so that the perfect dress looked just that, who corrected the ill-advised self-cut fringe and, of course, distracted her from her first heartbreak. They had argued, probably more than either of them would have liked, and Kimmie had hated her in the way that all teenagers hated their mothers. But she loved her more than she hated her. It was never real hate, just the type that is really love. One idiot not paying attention behind the wheel, and all of that was gone.

With a shiver, she wondered how long she had been standing there at the side of the soil-covered grave. The funeral had ended hours ago and she had hidden out of sight until the last lingering friend had gone. As she wriggled her toes in her sodden, squelchy shoes and pulled her thick wool coat more tightly around her, it struck her that this would probably be her last ever memory of this place where she had grown up.

Soon she would be on a train headed northbound, to live with her grandparents. They hadn't come to the funeral, too old for such a long trip, and in a strange way Kimmie was glad. She wanted to say goodbye to her old life on her own. With a wry little smile, she could almost hear her mum saying what she often did: 'Independent from the start, I swear you came out of me knowing better.'

Kimmie ran a tentative finger over the smooth marble of the headstone. Simple and classy; her mother would have approved. She let out a sigh and crouched down low to the soil, placing a hand-tied bunch of her mum's favourite daisies softly on the ground to say her last goodbye.

Two days later it was a sullen, pale-faced girl who sat on the train, but the tears were gone. Her stony expression was at odds with the peaceful green of the sweatshirt she wore, her knees pulled up to her chest as if she was trying to block the world out with her legs. In front of her was an untouched sandwich, an upside down book and a bottle of water. The only movement she made was to casually twist a strand of black hair between her thumb and forefinger. The man opposite her wondered what the story behind her sad face was, but his stilted chitchat early in the journey had been met with a polite nod, so he left her to her thoughts. Kimmie stared out of the window as the hours passed, watching the terrain change to the soundtrack of the chugging engine.

It was an icy-cold greeting when she finally stepped on to the platform at her destination. The very north of Canada would be her new home. An old couple dressed in thick, warm coats were winding their way towards her, their faces etched with anxiety. She managed to summon a cracked half smile as they reached her.

'Welcome, love,' said her grandma, enveloping her in a comfortable hug which smelled of soap and milky tea.

She hugged back, but only just, not able to risk more tears. She untangled herself from the embrace, only to be pulled into a second one, this time with her grandfather, who spoke in a voice so low that it was almost a whisper, 'We're so glad you're here.'

Of course, they had lost her mum too. Kimmie had become all they had. She refused their offer to help with her battered suitcase but conceded to let her grandfather take the holdall, and her grandma, the canvas shopping bag which held her favourite books. The three of them made their way to the truck, crunching across the snow-laden car park. As they loaded what was left of Kimmie's belongings, she took a longing look towards the train which could take her back to where she'd come from. But then, as the Sun painted the mountains and licked the trees, she realised with a sharp breath, how beautiful it was here.

Her grandparents' home was cosy and welcoming and everywhere she looked Kimmie could see little bits of her mother tucked into unexpected places. Well-loved cushions and vintage china sat at odds with quirky pottery and expressive paintings.

'Did she make this?' she asked, pointing at a vibrant, but crudely made, collage on the wall.

'Yes,' said her grandmother, smiling from her eyes. 'She loved to make art, even as a little girl.'

'I know.'

The words came out bitter, twisted and angry but her grandmother was not deterred, continuing with a warm smile. 'She was always so proud of our Cree culture and she loved to share our stories through her pictures.'

Kimmie felt a little stab of guilt. Her mum had tried to share those stories with her too and as a little girl she had sat enthralled while they plaited each other's hair and her mother unravelled tale after historical tale. Then she got older; boys had caught her eye and there were friends to spend time with. Her logical little brain had embraced science and she had closed out her heritage. Letting out a little sigh, she excused herself, retreating to her bedroom where she could be alone with her thoughts and the

sound of the trees rustling in gentle conspiracy outside the window.

The weeks passed and life went on. Everyone had said it would and that proved to be the case. Not the life Kimmie expected, or even wanted, but life all the same. She started a new school, but made no friends. Most of the kids avoided the angry quiet girl with dead eyes who showed as little interest in them as they did in her. After school it was the same story. Kimmie would go for long walks on her own or sit and read alone in her room, leaving her anxious grandparents sitting downstairs wondering how they could help her cope with her grief and fearing that they would never get inside her head.

Several weeks after the move, Kimmie went for her daily walk much later than usual. She had grown to love the snowy terrain and cold stillness of the air. She pulled on her mittens and thrust her hands deep into her pockets, taking in a refreshing breath of the icy air. She felt free from her worries when she was outside with the ground bathed in moonlight. It always made the snow seem as if it was made up of millions of tiny flecks of glitter. It was a crisp, clear night and the lack of clouds made the stars brighter than usual. She sat on a rock and turned her face upwards to pick them out, as she often did. Soft, downy snowflakes drifted down to her upturned face, landing on her cold cheeks and gathering on her black eyelashes.

Then something magical happened.

At first it looked like cloud, a shimmering curtain of cloud; ethereal and pretty. As Kimmie watched, the cloud slowly took on a green hue and moved gracefully across the sky. Softly, slowly, it moved and her eyes refused to look away from this beautiful vision pinpricked by stars shining through the coloured display. The streak of subtle green became more and more vivid as it danced seamlessly from one shape to another, constantly changing. It seemed to Kimmie that although the changes were fast, they were in slow motion, all at the same time. For a while she wasn't a girl sitting on a log, but part of the nature around her, her breath moving with the lights above her in the sky.

She sat there until she was so cold she couldn't feel her hands or toes. Her heart felt lighter than it had since her mum died and she couldn't wait to share what she had seen with her grandparents.

Her hand had barely touched the handle of the creaky wooden back door, when it flew open and she saw the worry on her grandmother's face.

'Oh thank goodness!' Kimmie was swept into her bosom, the force of her embrace almost suffocating.

'What's the matter?' she asked, in genuine surprise.

'I thought you'd run away!'

'Where would I go?'

A low, throaty chuckle interrupted their exchange.

'I told her not to panic, you wouldn't have gone far. Besides …,' her grandfather paused to puff on his pipe, 'no

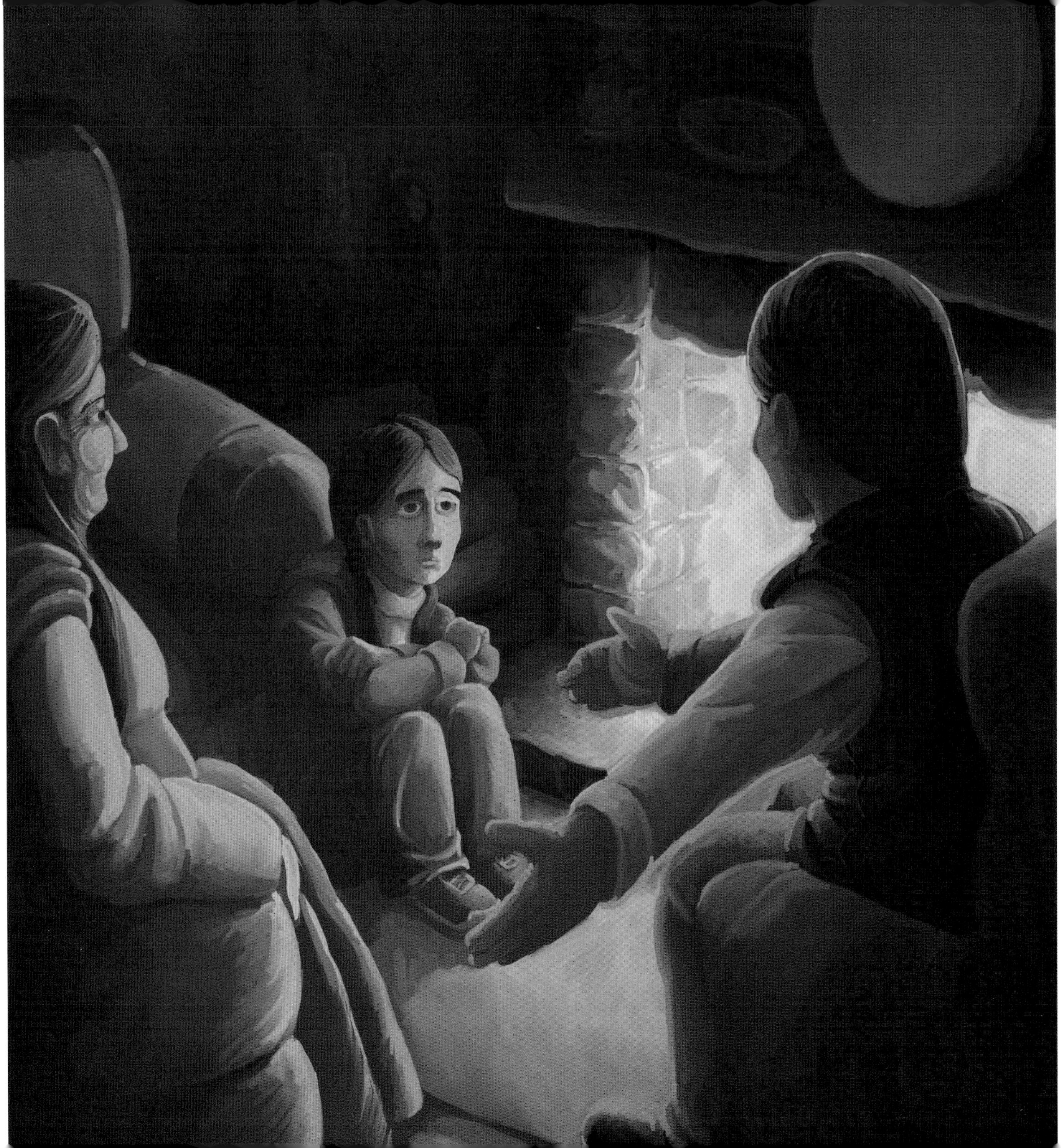

trains out of here this late.' He winked at her in cheeky conspiracy, just like her mum used to.

For the first time, Kimmie smiled a genuine deep smile that lit up her face and reached her eyes.

'I'm sorry you worried. I just lost track of time.'

Kimmie took her gloves off and went over to crouch by the fire, letting the orange flames warm her cold skin as they licked against the logs with a comforting crackle.

'It will be the lights you saw that made you lose track.'

'Yes!' Kimmie looked at her grandfather. 'The green ones: how did you know?'

He leaned toward her, close enough that Kimmie could smell coffee and tobacco on his breath, 'What else is there to see at night?'

Kimmie let out a little chuckle. She had not noticed how much like her mother he was. Her grandparents looked at each other in amusement, glad that their granddaughter was starting to emerge from the angry shell she had become since losing her mother.

'The aurora borealis I suppose,' continued Kimmie, staring into the hypnotic flames of the open fire, unaware of the joy on their faces. 'I knew you could see them from further north, I just didn't expect to.'

'Yes, on a clear night they are quite the sight,' her grandfather agreed, sitting back in his chair.

'And perhaps you needed to see them?' offered her grandmother gently.

'What do you mean?' Kimmie turned to look at her, her face furrowed with a frown as she allowed her hand to be enclosed by a softer, well-worn one.

'Well,' said her grandmother, 'have you learned all about the aurora borealis at school and the science that explains it?'

'Yes,' agreed Kimmie, 'of course.'

'That's all well and good, but the Cree people we are descended from had their own explanation for it.' She coughed, and then allowed a brief silence to wash over the three of them before continuing. 'The Cree used to call the lights the "Dance of the Spirits".'

Her grandfather picked up the story. 'They believed that the lights were a sign that loved ones they have lost are close, watching them and dancing for them to make them happy.'

He paused, watching her face. 'Isn't that nicer than science?'

'It is nicer. Not very logical, but much nicer.'

The three of them sat there together in comfortable silence enjoying the fire and Kimmie realised that whatever the science was, she had felt her mother tonight in a way she had longed to since losing her. So maybe, just maybe, it was her mother up there, dancing with the other spirits, to remind her that she wasn't alone, and that she was loved. And sitting there with the grandparents who loved her and desperately wanted her to be happy, Kimmie finally realised that even without her mother here with her, that was still true.

Photograph taken by Adam Shoker
from the Aurora Sky Station, Sweden.

7

SÁMI CULTURE

Sámi communities have lived under the Northern Lights for thousands of years, across parts of northern Norway, Finland, Sweden and the Kola peninsula of Russia, an area known as Sápmi.

Nithya Sivashankar. Illustrations by Aiden Whittam

The Sámi people are the indigenous people of Scandinavia. Traditionally, their community groups lived in small settlements or as nomadic groups. They have their own languages and religion, for which they were persecuted by other Scandinavian people for many years. The Sámi even had their own currency, *tjoervie*.

They are the only group from the area currently recognised and protected under the International Convention of Indigenous Peoples, although most of the Sámi population is now integrated more or less completely into modern society. It is estimated that there are around 60,000 Sámi people living in Sápmi today, for many of whom key aspects of their rich and interesting culture remain central to their way of life.

Culinary culture

Unlike the Gregorian calendar, the Sámi year consists of thirteen months and eight seasons. Most Sámi calendars are influenced by the life-cycle of the reindeer, and the weather conditions. In turn, the seasons affect the food habits of the Sámi people. Owing to the reindeer migration and their traditional nomadic lifestyle, the Sámi generally tend to preserve their food to last for days. Salting, drying and smoking are the preferred forms of preservation.

In the late winter, when the migration of the reindeer towards the west begins, the herders carry with them their staple food; of dried reindeer meat and blood pancakes (dried reindeer blood mixed with water, flour and salt, and cooked over fire). While cooked fish and a soup made of dried meat

Apart from the seasonal dishes, sautéed reindeer (made out of shoulder meat) and gáhkku (a type of bread baked over the lavvu fire) are some of the best known traditional meals from the Sápmi region.

Nowadays, reindeer hamburgers are served in fast-food restaurants in Sápmi.

A traditional Sámi food hut, a 'nili', would be raised on stilts to prevent animals from getting into the food supply. The food could only be reached by using a short, hand-made ladder. A nili would be built from wood and might have mud packed into any gaps to keep the wind and snow out. Though the nili is not always successful in keeping wildlife at bay ...

Photograph taken by Adam Shoker in Abisko National Park, Sweden.

are associated with the onset of spring, and calving in May, summer foods include pinewood-bark bread, cloudberries, smoked fish, soups made from the Angelica plant, and a porridge made out of juobmu, a popular herb.

The reindeer, which have grazed the green pastures over summer, begin their journey back to the forests towards the end of the season. This is the period when the herders slaughter the animals. A grand stew made using every imaginable part of the reindeer is prepared during this season. When autumn, the main harvesting season for the Sámi, sets in, lingonberries; raspberries; crowberries; and

bilberries abound. This season is important for fishing, as well as moose and bird hunting.

Before the arrival of winter, the reindeer meat is treated to prevent rotting. The meat is left hanging for days on top of the lavvu and is smoked all day long from a fire built in the tents. Following this, the meat is salted, cold smoked and preserved. As Christmas approaches, the herders are ready for the second round of slaughtering, during which the females and the calves are usually butchered, and their blood is collected to prepare blood bread. The blood is whisked with salt, flour and fat to a thick, porridge-like consistency,

Left An artist's impression of a 'nili'.

and boiled to produce chunky pieces. Blood bread is usually served with butter and lingonberry jam.

Trades

Traditionally, the Sámi people are involved in reindeer husbandry, although nowadays many of them branch out into tourism, art and designing, food production, and small-scale entrepreneurial ventures.

Reindeer herding forms a core part of the Sámi culture and their identity, so much so that their lifestyle is immensely influenced by the animals and their migration. The Sámi people are the last reindeer herders in the world, and herding has been their primary occupation for thousands of years. Although they faced several threats, such as racism, modernization, tourism, and other government policies, over the years, herding has withstood time and evolved in the recent past. From skis and herding dogs to snowmobiles, helicopters and mobile communications, technological advancements have played a crucial role in the development of the trade industry.

Duodji (the act of using hands to create something), an integral part of the Sámi culture, is another one of the main occupations of the inhabitants of Sápmi. Due to their nomadic lifestyle, the Sámi were forced to make their own utensils and tools, such as knives, for survival. The men were in charge of the 'hard handicrafts' (those made with wood and horn) while the women took care of the 'soft' ones (sewing using skins and roots). The fur, antlers, bones, tendons and skin of the reindeer were used as raw materials in the past, and craftsmen continue to use them in the present day. As with most of the primary occupations of the Sámi, Duodji is also influenced by the seasons. The craftsmen spend the winter months processing the raw materials. In spring, they set out to collect materials such as birch roots and Angelica for dyeing purposes. In September, the 'slaughter month', the reindeer tendons and hides are collected and prepared for the coming year.

Some of the traditional Sámi handicrafts include storage containers, made out of tubers or birch burls, and the náhppi (a reindeer milking bowl). Nowadays, owing to the influence of tourism in the Sápmi, the Sámi handicrafts are considered as works of art rather than essential commodities. Sámi Duodji, a foundation established in 1993, trains the Sámi people in crafts and assists them in marketing their products.

Sámi language

Sámi, a collective term for the group of languages spoken by the Sámi people, is derived from the Uralic languages – those that are spoken on both the sides of the Ural mountains. Although the history of Sámi is unknown, it is believed that the Finnish and Sámi languages originate from the same protolanguage, Early Finno-Sámi. Around 1000 BC, Finno-Sámi branched out and gave rise to the Proto-Sámi language. By the ninth century AD, Proto-Sámi had further been sub-divided into the various Sámi dialects, some of which are used today.

Sámi can be divided into three categories: East Sámi – spoken by the people in the Kola Peninsula, Central Sámi – spoken by those in Sweden, Norway and Finland, and South Sámi – spoken in Sweden and Norway. Further sub-divisions give rise to many Sámi languages, nine of which are in use, while the rest are threatened with extinction.

It was not until 2002 that Sámi languages were given official status in Sweden and recognised as minority languages. Until 1956, children who attended schools in Sweden were punished if they used Sámi languages in school.

They were taught lessons in Swedish. In the present day, although most schools continue to provide education in the majority languages, there exist a few Sámi schools and other schools that offer teaching in Sámi.

Yoiking

Yoiking, which was at one time not even considered music, is now regarded as one of the oldest forms of music in Europe. Similar to the word 'Sámi', 'Yoik' is a collective term, and there are different yoiking dialects based on where the yoiker is from. The three main yoik dialects are Yuollie (southern Sámi Yoik), Luohti (northern Sámi Yoik) and Leu'dd (a traditional form of singing of the Skolt Sámis who live in the eastern-most part of the Sápmi).

The Sámi people believe that yoiking creates a bond between animals, nature and themselves. They consider yoiking spiritual. They state that the yoikers do not yoik about something, as singers do. Yoikers yoik a feeling, a place or a person, and they become part of what they are yoiking. In the past, every person had their own yoik and developed them as they grew older. Sometimes, the Sámi people yoik important events. They even yoik the dead as an act of remembrance.

Johan Turi, the first Sámi author to publish a book in

Photograph taken by Adam Shoker, Abisko, Sweden.

In 2004, for the first time, an award worth NOK 100,000 was instituted by Ministers for Sámi Affairs and presidents of the Sámi parliaments in Sweden, Norway and Finland, for the promotion and preservation of the Sámi language. Gollegiella, the biennial Nordic Sámi language prize, is awarded to individuals or organisations that have aided in the promotion and development of the language.

Sámi has evolved in recent decades, and many words have been found or loaned, but the number of Sámi speakers has dwindled considerably.

Did you know that there are over 300 words for 'snow' and 'ice', and as many as 1,000 words related to 'reindeer' in the Sámi language? Or that in Sámi there are over 40 different forms of a verb?

While 'Yoik' is used to denote the way the Sámi people sing, 'Lavlodh' is the term used for the western way of singing. Among the renowned Sámi yoiking artists are Wimme Saari, Mari Boine, Nils-Aslak Valkeapää, and Sofia Jannok.

In the late 1990s 'Shaman', a Finnish folk metal band, introduced the idea of 'Yoik metal' to promote Sámi music in the world of heavy metal. In their compositions they used yoiking, Sámi lyrics, and the shamanic drum.

Until recently Yoiking was a pastime often associated with drunkenness. This was because early traders in search of reindeer skins introduced alcohol to the Sámi.

Photograph taken by Adam Shoker in Abisko National Park, Sweden. The Lapporten, or *cunonjavaggi*, in Sámi, is a U-shaped landmark traditionally used by the Sámi for navigation when herding their reindeer, and which was considered to be a holy place.

the Sámi language writes: 'Yoiking is a way of remembering. Some are remembered in hate and in love, while others are remembered in sorrow.'

In the early seventeenth century, the king of Denmark and Norway proclaimed that yoiking was a form of witchcraft and the practitioners of this art form were condemned to death. There are still people who consider it offensive to yoik in a church.

Although yoiking did not receive much attention for many centuries, many young Sámi are reawakening the spirit of yoiking by integrating the music form with its more modern counterparts.

Hobbies

As with the other aspects of their lifestyle, the reindeer influence the sporting activities of the Sámi people. Reindeer sled races are a popular sport in the northern region of the Sápmi, as are herding contests. Held annually, they test the participants based on their lasso-throwing, rifle-handling, reindeer-racing and skiing abilities. It is believed that the Sámi people may have laid the foundation for skiing. In the late nineteenth century, Sweden witnessed the first ski races and the Sámi skiers emerged winners. In 1884, Nordenskiöld Race – claimed to be the first ski event to be organised in the world – was held in Jokkmokk, and it covered 220 km.

The second most popular sport among the Sámi people is football. The Swedish Sámi Sports Association and the Sámi Football Association are the two important sports organisations in the Sápmi. Sápmi National Football Team represents the Sámi people of Sweden, Norway, Finland and Russia, however since the team is not a member of UEFA or FIFA, the members do not take part in the events organised by these associations.

The biggest football tournament for the people from the Sápmi region is The Sámi Cup, which has been held since 1978. The tournament was set up to bring the disparate people from the different parts of Sápmi together. All Saints Cup, an indoor football championship held in Gällivare, is another important event for people from the different regions of Sápmi. Apart from this, there is also the South Sámi Cup, a football tournament for people from Norway and Sweden in Southern Sápmi.

A photograph from between 1900 and 1920, showing a group of Nordic Sámi people in Sápmi, with lavvu.

Photograph taken by Adam Shoker, from
the Aurora Sky Station, Abisko, Sweden.

8

SÁMI BELIEFS AND TRADITIONS

Linda Sever

Nature and the sacred landscape

Sámi tradition makes no great distinction between culture (that which is man-made) and nature (that which is not man-made); people and human activities are believed to be a part of nature. For instance, the Sámi have no word for 'wilderness', as all people and nature are equal, and so an area where there is wilderness but no human connection is an alien concept. Anthropologists have uncovered such belief patterns among many of the world's indigenous peoples, although it is still very important for the Sámi people even today.

The Sámi journey through nature was traditionally connected with usefulness, rather than just wandering or walking. 'Going for a walk' was not considered to be a normal activity. People went out to fish, hunt, tend herds of reindeer, or to see if the cloudberry plants had started to blossom. Whilst they were out they had to consider the many gods and forces believed to exist in nature. Many places were holy and had to be treated with respect, and for some this is still a living tradition.

Sáivu

The word 'sáivu' can mean various things, but it is often linked to another world, or worlds, and the beings that live there. In southern Sámi areas, saajve-vaerieh is the term used for the holy mountains, also known as the 'heritage mountains'. The spirits which inhabit these mountains are called saajve or saajve-ålmaj (sáivu people). It is these spirits that taught the noaidi: shamans and healers from the Sámi community. Sáivu has also been used to describe lakes or tarns with a double bottom. On the other side of the lake bed lay the sáivu realm, where everything was bigger and better than in the world of people. The fish in a sáivu lake were especially fine and fat, but could be difficult to catch. In pre-Christian times offerings were often made to sieidi in many sáivu lakes.

Artist's impression of a Sámi man, by Aiden Whittam.

Sámi faith and beliefs

The Sámi had an encompassing, 'polytheistic' faith, which meant there were no limits to the number of gods one could believe in.

The Sámi had many gods and rituals from other faiths they had come into contact with over the course of time. For example, both the Norse and the Sámi believed in the thunder god, Thor, who was one of the most important gods, particularly for men.

According to the old Sámi faith, there are gods and forces all around us in nature and in the home. In the past, making offerings to these forces was an everyday part of Sámi life.

Norse sagas tell of Sámi witchcraft. This was thought to be particularly powerful. In one saga, Gunnhild, the daughter of Ossur Tote of Hålogaland, was sent to two Sámi in Finnmark to learn witchcraft. There she met Eirik Bloodaxe, whom she married. Gunnhild became known as a woman very skilled in the art of witchcraft, which she used to influence politics. In the end she was killed, and sunk in a bog, by Håkon the Good.

Attempts were made to bring Christianity to the Sámi from as early as the fourteenth century, with the most intense missionary activity taking place in the seventeenth and eighteenth centuries, while the old faith was hidden, and partly forgotten. However, in spite of this, a number of traditions and beliefs regarding the old gods and spirits have survived. Certain rituals and parts of the Sámi faith and mythology have been preserved right up to the present day, and remain important parts of Sámi culture.

Shamanism

The old faith of the Sámi is often described as 'shamanistic'. This means that the faith is dependent on a spiritual leader, or a 'shaman'. The shaman enters an altered state of consciousness, or a type of trance, after eating a certain plant, or through drumming or rhythmic dance. Once in this trance the Shaman can communicate with the world of gods or spirits and bring back information for the community, who might ask questions about their relationships, health or financial and material issues.

Different forms of shamanism are found all over the world, especially among aboriginal peoples. The word 'shaman' comes from the Siberian languages. Among the Sámi these spiritual leaders have had several different names or labels, of which the most often used is 'noaidi'.

Gods, spirits and other beings

Gods, spirits and other beings were important in Sámi faith and mythology. The most important gods varied from place to place, and also over the course of time. The same god could have several names and different characteristics depending on the location. On the following pages is a list of the best known gods, spirits and other beings found in seventeenth- and eighteenth-century sources:

Árja	A female 'gazzi' or ancestor spirit. The name means 'energy', 'decisiveness'.
Bárbmoáhkká	Ensures that all migratory birds return from warmer countries.
Beaivi/Biejvve/Biejjie	The name for the Sun. Sun worship was very important in Sámi religion and was a form of fertility cult.
Bieggaalmmái	The 'wind man' decided the wind direction, which was particularly important for reindeer hunting.
Boaššuáhkká	The goddess who brought about success in hunting.
Čáhcealmmái/Tsjaetsieålmaj	The 'water man', who ruled over lakes and fishing.
Čahcerávga/Guovdi	Lived in rivers or the sea, and was used to scare children as part of bringing them up.
Čahkálakkat	These small, naked creatures lived near springs. Their heads had the power to heal and their stomachs were full of silver coins. These benefits could be obtained by tricking and killing them.
Fásto-olmmái	'The fast man', who told the Sámi to observe fasting days.
Gieddegeašgálgu	A wise female being who lived on the edge of people's dwelling places, and who could be approached when life was especially difficult. More recently gieddegeašgálgu has acquired the more negative meaning, 'old gossip'. This belief originated in northern Sámi areas.

Gufihtar	These spirits lived inside a hill or mound called a gufihtarčohkka. They would lure children into their mounds, which the children would not be able to leave if they were to eat or drink while in there.
Guolleipmil	The 'fishing god' ruled over fishing. Many places of offering beside lakes, tarns and rivers are called Guolleipmil.
Hálddit	Protected animals and plants and ruled of areas of nature.
Ipmel/Ibmil/Jubmel/Jupmele	Some noaidis believed that Raedieaehtjie (the highest god – see below) and Raediegiedtie (son of the highest god) were the same, namely Ipmel/Ibmil. He was regarded as the highest ranking god. With the coming of Christianity, missionaries adopted the name Ipmel/Ibmil, and it became the Sámi name for the Christian God.
Jábmiidáhkká/Jábbmeáhkká/ Jaemiehaahka	The goddess of the dead, who held authority over the realm of the dead, Jábmiidáibmu.
Jámiš	The dead who lived beneath the earth.
Joeksaahka/Juksáhkká	The goddess of the bow or childbirth. She lived in boaššu – the sacred part of a dwelling, behind the fireplace. She was believed to be involved when children were created, and had the ability to transform the unborn child into a boy.
Kirvaradien/Tjåervieraeie	The 'horn ruler'.

Leaibealmmái/Liejbålmaj/ Liejpålmaj	The 'alder tree man' was god of the hunt, ruled over the wild animals of the forest, and accepted offerings before a bear hunt, made to protect the hunters. The alder tree was considered sacred; the red colour from its bark was used to paint drums, and the juice was sprayed over returning bear hunters.
Mailmenraedie: Máilbmi + raedie	Rulers of the world.
Maadteraahkas/Máhtáráhkká	'Primal mother' or 'great grandmother', was mother of the three goddesses Sáhráhkká, Juksáhkká and Uksáhkká. She was believed to be involved when children were created.
Noaidegázzi/sáivugázzi, noaidegadze/saivogadze (Gázzi)	These were helper spirits; their names might be translated as 'followers' or 'companions'. They often looked like small people clad in colourful Sámi clothes. It is possible that they were regarded as ancestor spirits. They would choose people to be trained as noaidis (shamans) whom they would accompany for the rest of their lives, including on journeys to search for souls. Gázzi could also be inherited or form part of a dowry.
Noaideloddi/sáivoloddi, noaideguolli/sáivoguolli and noaidesarvvis/sáivosarvvis	The noaidis also had helper spirits in animal form. They might be birds (noaideloddi/ sáivoloddi), fish (noaideguolli/sáivoguolli), or reindeer bucks (noaidesarvvis/sáivosarvvis). The most powerful noaidis had reindeer bucks as their animal helpers.
Oksaahka/Uhksáhkká	The 'door goddess', who lived under the door sill and protected a dwelling against all evil. Her role was to look out for children during their first year, especially when they were learning to walk.
Radien kieddi/Raediegiedtie	Raedieaehtjie's son.
Radien-acce/-attje/Raedieaehtjie	The highest god, the primal father, the highest.

Rohttu	The god of sickness and death, who lived in a dismal realm of the dead, Rohttuáibmu.
Ruđot	Female gázzi beings. The name could mean 'bringing the sound of moaning'.
Serge-edni	Raedieaehtjie or Ipmel's wife. She could create a human spirit and would convey it to Máthuráhkká when children were created.
Stállu	Giant or troll-like figure. He was used to scare children into behaving, during their upbringing.
Storjunkeren	Ruled over wild animals, birds and fish. Looked on as the deputy of the highest god Tiermes.
Saajve/Saajveolmai, Saivo/ Saivo-olmai	Spirits linked to holy mountains, also called saajve or 'heritage mountains'. Those who owned saajve had helper animals at their service, see below.
Saaraahka/Sáhráhkká	Important goddess in southern Sámi areas, who lived beneath the fireplace. She received offerings of anything that could be drunk. She was important when children were created, and helped women with menstruation and childbirth. Children were baptised in the name of Sáráhkká.
Tiermes/Dierpmis/Bájanolmmái/ Aijeke/Átjek/Horagalles/ Hovrengaellies/Thor	Different names for the god of thunder, who ruled over people's lives and deaths. He was considered the most important god for men, and was symbolised by a hammer or a bow, the rainbow. He could call forth thunder, kill trolls, help in revenge, and prevent unwelcome visits.
Ulddat	Underground beings in human form, who lived in special mountains.

Sámi mythology

All cultures have myths about creation and why the world is the way it is. The Sámi are no different. They have many different myths about the gods, the creation of the world and humans, and why they keep reindeer. For example, there is a myth about how the Sun proposed in the land of the giants or 'Peiverbarnen suongah jehtasnsan maajisn'. This myth tells of how the son of the Sun met and married a giant's daughter, and what this means for Sámi people today, which you can read about on page 69.

The creation myth; 'Jubmel and Berkel and the creation of the humans'

At Kaitum in Gällivare, Sweden, the Sámi believed that Jubmel, the god of the sky, had created the world together with the evil Berkel. Jubmel wanted all trees to be made of marrow and all lakes to be made of milk, but Berkel prevented this. So the world was not as Jubmel desired.

Before the world was formed as it is today by Jubmel and Berkel, there had been a great flood. All people except a boy and a girl were drowned. Jubmel led the boy and girl to the safety of a high mountain, Bassevare, the holy mountain. When the danger was over they each went in a different direction to search for other people. They met again after three years, without having found anyone else. Three times this happened, but upon their third meeting they did not recognise each other. This time they stayed together, and had children. From their union, it was believed, came all the people of the world.

Myths about why the Sámi keep reindeer

A southern Sámi tradition holds that the Sámi originally wanted to have the elk as their animal. But the elk always stayed around the turf huts and never left the Sámi in peace. An old woman prayed that they could have an animal which ran away from the turf hut, so the kids had something to do, and so the Sámi got the reindeer instead.

In other places the Sámi believed that the elk belonged to Biejjen nieide, the Sun's daughter. One day she was captured by a man and went with him to his lavvu. The Sun's daughter told him he could keep both her and the elk if he could stay in the lavvu for three nights with the smoke hole and the opening at the back of the tent covered up. He managed it for two nights, but on the third he lifted the covering on the smoke hole, because he did not think it was any great risk. 'Mu attjen ja tittjen tjalmeh vuoinoh!' shouted the Sun's daughter – 'Now you can see my father's and my mother's eyes!' Then she disappeared up and out of the smoke hole, and neither she nor the tame elk ever came back.

Fables and folk tales

Sámi fables and folk tales often contain concepts originating from pre-Christian times. A number of fables and folk tales have been collected from various Sámi areas. The most important source is Just Qvigstad's four-volume work *Lappiske Eventyr og Sagn.*

The Sámi stories are about noaidis (noaidi) (shamans), the Chud (čuđit), animals, natural formations, offering sites, ghosts (jámiš), the Stallo (stállu), the Chakalaggs (čakalagat), spirits (háldit and gofihtar), outcasts (eáhparaš) and a number of other themes. Sámi folk tales are also constructed in a special way, which may be explained by the presence of shamanistic features in Sámi communities well into the twentieth century.

Fables and folk tales about Stállu and giants

Stállu was a scary creature. Today, we no longer know much it about today. He could be a man-eating monster, and it was believed that he could turn people into a Stállu. You could also send Stállu to someone you were mad at, as revenge.

It was believed that Stállu could move around people invisibly, where he collected silver items. To get to the silver you would have to kill both him and his dog. However, other times Stállu is described as bit stupid and easy to trick.

Stállu was often seen with his dog and if you heard whistling in the woods it could be Stállu blowing his whistle. In some tales they talk about 'jetter', or giants, instead of Stállus.

Sámi beliefs today

One of the rituals and traditions which survived the coming of Christianity in the 17th and 18th centuries is the respect for sacred places in the landscape. Certain holy mountains are still revered, for example by not referring to them by name.

Old offering sites and sieidi have not been entirely forgotten either. Offerings are still made, in the form of reindeer antlers, fish, berries, coins or other items. Some of those making offerings have living beliefs about the Sámi gods who belong to the place. For others the offering is a way of showing respect for their ancestors and their faith. Others place a small gift in passing, more out of habit than because of any special faith.

Mythical beings are still reality for some in Sámi areas. Many believe in the underground spirits and some say they have both seen and spoken to gufihttar. In some cases, figures of legend such as Stállu (troll/giant) and Čahcerávga or Guovdi (river spirits/sea monsters) are still used in the upbringing of children, to scare them into behaving properly and staying away from dangerous places.

During the last 50 years, shamanism has acquired new followers the world over. Many have approached the shamanistic faith in order to come into contact with other levels of consciousness, and perhaps to foretell the future, or to heal. This revival of interest has been dubbed the 'new shamanism'.

In order to achieve another state of consciousness, drums in particular are used, but also dance, song and other

66

methods. Some have used various intoxicants to achieve the desired effect.

Sámi shamanism, noaidevuohta, too has attracted new followers. The Sámi form of new shamanism is based on knowledge of the old faith, but it is debatable whether this new shamanism is really descended from the pre-Christian Sámi faith. It is a great leap, both in time and culture, from the last noaidis, part of a Sámi shamanistic society, to the individuals who wish to practise Sámi shamanism today.

Those who practise Sámi new shamanism believe that they are calling on a force which has always been accessible and that this in itself connects them with an ancient tradition. Some also point to kinship with actual noaidis from pre-Christian times.

Photograph taken by *Lights Over Lapland* photographer Chad Blakley. Exposure: 4.0 sec; f/2.8; ISO 1600.

Photograph taken by *Lights Over Lapland* photographer
Chad Blakley. Exposure: 6.0 sec; f/1.4; ISO 1600.

9

THE SON OF THE SUN

Some believe that the ancestors of the Sámi people are descended from giants who lived in a dark land to the far west of the Sun and the Moon.

Kathryn Blatch. Illustrations by Aiden Whittam

Long ago when the Earth was still young, there were very few womenfolk in the land of the Sun. As the Sun's son was of the age where he was expected to produce an heir, this caused some difficulties. The brave young man who possessed both fair looks and intelligence decided to travel abroad to find himself a pleasing young maiden to take as his wife.

There was a land to the west of the Sun and the Moon. It was fabled to be a land full of amazing treasures, with boulders of gold and silver lying upon its shores. However, it was also home to a tribe of fierce giants, who liked to feast on human flesh. Even so, the brave young hero could not be dissuaded from seeking a bride from such a daunting land. He was young, and naively assumed a maiden of any size would find his charm irresistible. Moreover, the appeal of glorious treasure outweighed the fear of unknown colossal beings and their dietary habits.

Thus, he engaged a crew of hearty men and set sail. The journey was hazardous, with storms and hurricanes. Many a time, his men's hearts grew doubtful and they urged the King's son to return home. After a full twelve months, land was sighted. They had, at last, arrived at the land beyond the Sun. It was the Land of Giants. It was a dark and dim land without the Sun to light its plains and mountains. In fact, it was rumoured that the Sun's rays were harmful to the giants that inhabited its shores.

The men dropped anchor and climbed down onto the strange shore, marvelling at the shining rocks of gold and silver. The Sun's son set eyes upon a maiden thrice as tall as he. Her hands were the size of reindeer haunches and her feet

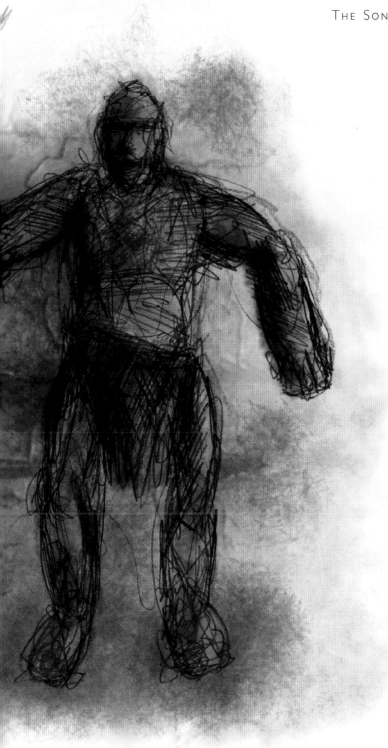

the length of his favourite hound, but she had soft eyes and dimples in her cheeks. He immediately felt a great tremor in his heart and knew at once he had found his bride.

The giant maiden asked him from where he came and whom he sought … and then if he would become meat for her family's table! The valiant youth did not flinch but replied that he was the son of a great king who was seeking a wife. She would be a handsome companion, would comfort him in times of trouble, would become a friend, and eventually a mother to his offspring. Upon hearing this, a warm rush of love filled the giant's heart and she consented to take this stranger as her husband.

This giantess, who looked after her ailing father and two brothers, would be sorely missed. Even so, she believed that her father could be persuaded to let her marry this stranger. The biggest problem would be her suitor's small stature but, as her father was blind, she was sure she could trick him into believing the son of the Sun was worthy of her hand. She knew that to win her in marriage he would have to defeat her father in a contest of strength, a feat she would help him to achieve.

The giant father challenged the son of the Sun to a finger bending contest to win his daughter's hand, as was tradition in this unusual land. As the blind giant father was so full of might, his daughter heaved an iron glove into her father's hand, in place of that of her suitor. The giant struggled to bend the young man's finger for many hours. To feed his great appetite, the old giant ate horsemeat and drank mead and was soon incapacitated. This robbed him even further of his strength and rendered him incapable of continuing the contest. Finally the giant agreed to their marriage, believing that the Son's people must be strong and sturdy.

A whale skin was laid upon the ground for the couple to step on. The bride's father cut wounds in their fingers and, after mingling their blood, they were husband and wife. Then he gave his daughter and her new husband a dowry of gold and silver to fill their ship. The giantess carried three beautiful wooden chests from her house aboard, and a wash cloth tied with three knots. Each knot could cause terrible effects: peace and strife; illness and plague; blood and fire. It would aid them in their journey from the Land of Giants.

Then the new bride urged her husband and his crew to make haste before her brothers returned from their day's labour. No sooner had she spoken, the earth beneath their feet started to shake, and terrible roars reached their ears. The three brothers had learned the news from their father and wanted to bring their sister back.

Just as their ship sailed from the shore, three colossal men appeared waving heavy silver spears over their heads. The giant brothers leapt into their boat and the loud creak of oars could soon be heard. In no time at all, they were upon the Sun's people. Their sister shook a knot from her wash cloth and a strong gust came from nowhere, pushing their boat far ahead of the vengeful giants.

The giants' hearts were full of ire, and this drove them to paddle with an almighty strength. Almost immediately, the Son's people could hear loud roars: the giant brothers were close behind. For a second time, the giantess shook a knot from her wash cloth. A powerful wind filled the sails and carried their boat on with great speed.

Nevertheless, the giants' thirst for vengeance drove them on more powerfully still. With sweat and toil, they got within thumping distance of their sister's boat. Full of terror, the crew called for their master's wife to save them.

This time, the giantess-bride loosened her last knot and a great storm shook the mast and ripped the sails. Huge rolling waves lifted the boat, taking it a long distance from the giants. As sunrise drew near, the defeated brothers landed ashore. They climbed high to try and spot their sister's boat among the waves. Just at that moment, the Sun lit up the dark land and shot forth hot, white beams, instantly turning the giants into stone. These tall mountains still stand today, keeping watch for their sister's return.

The happy couple returned to the Land of the Sun where they held a second wedding ceremony, and by stepping upon soft reindeer skin, the giantess shrank to human size. The married pair lived a long and happy life, producing many fine children known as the Galla-bartnet. These are the ancestors of the Sámi people; the stars who shine down upon them each night from the heavens.

10

LOOKING FOR LOTTA

The Sámi believed that the Northern Lights represented the spirits of their ancestors, and that if you made any noise while in the presence of the ethereal phenomenon it would whisk you away – a fate only preventable by whistling.

Kathryn Blatch. Illustrated by Mick McLaren

Gunnar slumped by the fire. The heat warmed him to his bones, melting away the exhaustion. It had been a busy and exhilarating day. The group of Sámi herders had found grazing grounds where the herds would be safe from wolves, and where there was plenty of moss under the snow for them to eat. Now everyone could relax.

He glanced across to where Hanna was sitting, with firelight glinting in her eyes. From behind her dark curtain of hair he sensed she was smiling. She was no longer a friend to him but a beautiful and mysterious creature. She was petite, with jet black hair as dark as a starless sky. She had strong hands, though, and he knew she was skilful with the reindeer.

Gunnar felt the heat rush to his face and tried, and failed, to stop a daft grin spreading there. He turned away from the fire, pretending to check out his father's herd, to hide his darkened cheeks. Before he could turn back to sneak a look at Hanna, he felt a tug at his jacket sleeve. A young sturdy girl with a mass of untidy hair stood next to him. 'Gunnar, come play with me!'

He glared at her, 'Lotta, why did you leave the tent? Father will be cross.'

'I don't like being on my own.'

'Go back to bed, Lotta. It's late.'

Gunnar felt Hanna's eyes on them. He looked over expecting her to be amused, but she shot him a sympathetic look that made him relent.

'Okay, you can play until the embers burn low.'

'Thank you!'

His sister shot off towards a gaggle of children chasing each other at the edge of the camp.

He shrugged his shoulders at Hanna and she smiled. After that, the shyness disappeared and soon Hanna and Gunnar were sitting side by side, catching up on what had happened since the last winter camp together. Gunnar wondered if she had a young man, but surely she would not be sitting so close if she had. This thought lit up his heart and quickly moved Lotta to the back of his mind.

Suddenly Gunnar became aware that theirs were the only voices audible around the campfire. He nudged Hanna. Everyone was silent, looking up at the pulsing sky; the spirits of their Sámi ancestors were ascending to heaven. Jade swirls of light rolled slowly across the inky sky. There was not a human voice to be heard. A loud shout of laughter suddenly burst forth, and Gunnar recognised it at once. His chest tightened and, as if he had wings, he flew towards Lotta to silence her.

Before he could reach her, Lotta was snatched by invisible hands and dragged up into the pulsing jade clouds. She soared high above Gunnar's head. 'Lotta!' he screamed, not caring now if he angered the spirits, 'Lotta!' Later, he could not forgive himself for forgetting to clap his hands loudly before it was too late – he had been too full of fear and trepidation to remember what his father had taught him.

He had promised his mother on the day she died that he would look after his sister. Now he had let down both his mother and Lotta. He gazed up at the heavens and vowed, 'I will find you, Lotta, and I will bring you home.'

The next morning, before his father had awoken, Gunnar crept out of their lavvu. He hadn't told his father about Lotta being snatched by the Northern Lights and wanted to sort it out quickly, before he found out on his own. Gunnar hoped that his father would think the two of them were out together, checking on the herd. Gunnar had no idea how to tell his dad, but believed that some good news from the Noiadi, a shaman, would help. The Noaidi's drumming hadn't been able to save his mother but, maybe, just maybe, he could help him find Lotta.

The Noaidi's lavvu was pitched a little way away from the camp, next to a sacred rock. Gunnar saw grey smoke swirling up from the opening at the top of the tent – he was in luck, the Noiadi was awake. He called gently, and the Noaidi came to the tent's entrance to let Gunnar inside. As he started to tell the tale of Lotta's disappearance the Noaidi closed his eyes, and nodded from time to time. Towards the end of Gunnar's story he held up his hands for silence and went to fetch the familiar, oval Shaman drum made from reindeer hide. Gunnar looked at the drawings covering the drum and thought he spotted a reindeer, a horse and a bear. The Noaidi placed part of a reindeer antler on the drum and began to beat it and chant. The antler began to move around the drum, finally lying still on the bear – the Sacred One.

The Noaidi told Gunnar what he must do and, as Gunnar left the tent, his mind was occupied with the journey ahead. It would be difficult and challenging, he knew, but if it brought Lotta back to them it would be worth all the risk.

Later that morning, Gunnar left the camp with a bag full of food, a flask and a reindeer hide for warmth. He skied to the edge of the camp, turning back to see what he was leaving behind. He saw the lavvu with swirling plumes of smoke, children running and shrieking, and there in the distance his father, Erk, looking lost and lonely, collecting firewood – Lotta's job. Gunnar sniffed, hitched his bag more securely onto his shoulders and tightened his skis. If he had looked for just a moment longer he might have spotted the dark-haired girl, making her way towards him.

After skiing for several hours up the hill, Gunnar found a flat rock to rest on. He had just finished his meal when Hanna appeared, as if from nowhere.

'What are you doing Hanna? We talked about this.'

'I told you this morning and I'm telling you now – I'm responsible too.'

'It's not safe. Go back to the camp.'

'I'm coming with you! We can either go together or I can follow behind. But either way, you are not stopping me.'

'OK, if you're sure. But we need to hurry …'

Gunnar pointed to the dripping icicles and the green shoots poking through the snow. Spring was on its way, and soon it would be time to move the reindeer on, to the summer grazing grounds.

When dusk began to fall, Gunnar and Hanna found shelter under a grove of trees. They swept some of the snow away, built a fire, laid the thick reindeer hides on the ground, and huddled together for warmth. Gunnar had not felt so at peace since he was a child in his mother's arms. He felt her soft lips against his mouth and they kissed at last. They held on to each other tight, as if afraid they would lose one another.

In the grey morning light, Hanna and Gunnar set off once again. Their journey lasted many days, each much the same as the last. Finally, they came to a raging river, swollen with melting snow. It was much too wide to cross.

'What will we do now?' Gunnar asked.

'Let's ask Galggo.' suggested Hanna.

They began to look around the meadow for signs of this helpful spirit. They found a tree full of blossom, even though Spring had not yet arrived in that part of Sápmi. They offered some of their dried meat and asked Galggo for help. The tree began to shake, though there was no wind. When they looked down, the fallen blossoms had formed an arrow pointing to the west, back the way they had come. There would be no need to cross the river after all!

They followed the direction of the arrow with their eyes and could see, high up in the mountains, the dark mouth of a cave. Isavoi, the Sacred One, would be taking his long winter slumber there. Gunnar explained to Hanna that the Noaidi had instructed him to beg the Sacred One to mediate with the Sky Gods on his behalf. This had never been done before and it was possible that the bear would attack him instead. He had been told that the journey was going to be hazardous, and he would need to keep his wits about him.

When they were almost at the mouth of the cave Gunnar turned to his companion: 'Hanna, promise me you'll stay here, no matter what you hear or see, OK?' It was forbidden for Sámi women to look upon the Sacred One while it was alive, so she agreed. Hanna went to sit behind a large rock, her mind full of fear.

Gunnar approached the cave entrance, cautiously creeping into the darkness. He stood for a while and listened, sniffing the air. He could hear the soft breathing of Muottat – the fur clad one – and could smell its rancid odour. As he moved further into the darkness he stumbled on the rock-strewn floor. His spear clattered to the ground and he turned pale as his pulse throbbed loudly in his ears. He stayed focused on the creature, which had opened its eyes. Clouds of steam puffed from its nostrils with every breath, its body heavy after a long winter's sleep.

It glowered at Gunnar. A fierce growl echoed through the gloomy cave and Gunnar shuddered at the white glint of enormous teeth. He knew it was hopeless. The creature could rip out his throat with his fearsome claws before he could even pick up his spear. He dropped to his knees, bowing his head low. 'Oh Sacred One, I have gifts for you.' Watching the bear, he slowly withdrew offerings of dried reindeer meat and antlers from his bag, laying them between himself and the bear.

The Sacred One didn't speak, but Gunnar knew that all creatures could understand the Sámi people. His mind was suddenly filled with images that became words. 'Why should I help the puny human that disturbs my long slumbers?'

'I am sorry, Muottat, but I really need your help.'

The bear scraped the rock with huge claws, snatching the offerings. He carried them back to his bed of leaves in the

corner of the cave. After satisfying his hunger he stared at Gunnar, but this time his brown eyes were gentle and his breathing steady. 'Tell me what you want.'

'I would like you to ask to the Spirits of the Sky to return my sister.'

'And why should I do that?' was the next image-thought to form in Gunnar's head.

Gunnar explained what had happened that night, and how he believed it was his fault that his sister had been snatched away, as he had not been watching. The bear gave him a long, baleful stare and closed its eyes.

Gunnar tried as hard as he could to make word-pictures materialise in his head, but none came. He waited silently, praying for an answer. The rocks underfoot dug into his soles. He felt the icy wind rattle right through his reindeer hide, and drips of freezing water fall from the roof of the cave down the back of his neck. Was it a wasted journey? Had the creature gone back to its slumber? Gunnar's shoulders sagged and a great exhaustion came over him.

Just as the Sun was going down the creature opened its eyes, for a fraction of a second. A new message formed in Gunnar's mind: 'Go now, young human. All will be fine, return to your family.' He crawled out of the cave backwards, picked up his spear, and ran down the hill to Hanna's waiting arms before the beast could change its mind.

Hanna was peering at him through the brass ring, as all Sámi women did for a bear hunter. Gunnar snatched it from her explaining that all had gone well and he had left the Sacred One sleeping peacefully. They made their way back to camp, stopping very little as new buds were quickly forming on the trees, and the snow was melting fast.

By the time they reached the last slope they had to put away their skis, as the snow had gone completely. They stumbled down the hill, exhausted, and as they came around the last bend they were met with an unwelcome surprise: the herd and all the tents had gone! They quickly surveyed the scene, and suddenly spotted smoke coming from a distant fire, and two figures beside it – an adult, and a child with a mass of unruly hair that he recognised even from that distance. It could only mean one thing – Lotta was back! A huge grin spread across Gunnar's face. Grabbing Hanna's hand, he loped down the hill as fast as his legs could take him, dragging a giggling Hanna along by the arm.

They soon set off to catch up with the other herders, and Erk told his son not to press Lotta for details until she was ready to talk about her experience. At the camp, Gunnar and Lotta walked over to see their herd. Gunnar glanced down at his sister, trotting along at his side, and shuddered. He couldn't bear to think what could have happened to her. He grabbed her hand, feeling the tiny bones under her flesh.

'I'm so sorry, Lotta,' he said, for what must have been the hundredth time.

'Don't be!' she said gazing up at him. 'At first I was terrified, but I had an amazing time.'

'An amazing time?'

'Well, I met … our mother.'

'Our mother?'

'Yes! A beautiful woman hugged me and I knew it was her. She told me she was proud of me and loved us both very much. She also told me that I would return to the Earth because of my brother's love and courage.'

Gunnar felt the sense of guilt that had been weighing heavy on his chest shatter into tiny pieces and vanish.

He could breathe again.

'Were you sad to leave? Did you want to come back?'

'Not at first, but then mama told me about my new nephews and nieces that would join our family.' Lotta gave her brother a wide grin.

'Our new nephews and …?' Suddenly Gunnar understood what Lotta meant. He felt his cheeks redden but couldn't keep the smile from his face.

PHOTOGRAPHING THE AURORA: AN INSIDER'S GUIDE

by Lights Over Lapland photographer Chad Blakley, professional photographer and owner of Lights Over Lapland, a company offering Northern Lights photography tours in Abisko National Park, Sweden.

Photograph taken by *Lights Over Lapland* photographer Chad Blakley. Exposure: 6.0 sec; f/2.8; ISO 1600.

Photographers are a very special group of people. We spend countless hours online researching camera equipment, invest large quantities of our hard-earned cash into the latest and greatest gear, and go to unimaginable lengths to look for that perfect light with one goal in common: to capture a moment in time that will never be seen again.

One of nature's most spectacular displays of light is the often elusive, and technically challenging, aurora borealis. Aurora photography and tourism have gained a lot of attention in the last few years, and this new interest has caused countless aspiring aurora photographers to contact me and ask for a few pointers to help them succeed when chasing the lights.

A view of the aurora borealis from the ski lift at the Aurora Sky Station, Abisko National Park, Sweden. Taken by *Lights Over Lapland* photographer Chad Blakley. Exposure: 6.0 sec; f/2.8; ISO 1600.

A quick summary of my best advice ...

You will need the right camera if you are going to capture high-quality images, so always use a modern digital SLR camera. Pocket compact cameras, even high-end models, will not provide satisfactory results. If you don't have one, it's worth checking if you can hire one from an online camera rental service or an aurora photography outfitter.

Get familiar with the ISO settings on your camera. You will be shooting the aurora in low light situations and you will therefore need to use a high ISO. I generally recommend 800–1600 ISO for all exposures, unless you are using an extremely fast lens such as an f1.4.

Using the right lens is just as important as using the right camera. If possible try to use a fast, wide angle lens. A minimum aperture of f3.5 will work, but f2.8 or faster is recommended. An 18mm lens is a good minimum starting point.

A stable tripod is a must! You will need to use a long exposure to capture the lights, and if you try to do this by hand you'll only get blurry results. Forget about inexpensive, low-quality tripods as they often fail under the extremely cold conditions present above the Arctic Circle. It's worth checking if you can hire a suitable tripod on arrival.

A relatively inexpensive pro-tip is to invest in a wireless release for your camera. This lets you take a photograph without touching the camera and works best when the camera's shutter needs to stay open for a long duration, and you want to eliminate all possibility of camera shake. I recommend a wireless remote control device, because cable releases can become hard and brittle in the extreme cold north of the Arctic Circle.

Be sure to prepare for the effect that the Arctic climate will have on your camera equipment. You'll need to bring several extra batteries as they will function approximately one-third as long as they would under normal conditions. It would also be a good idea to invest in a high-quality memory card – all your prep will be for nothing if you have a cheap memory card, as they can become sluggish and fail in the cold conditions.

A headlamp with the option of a red beam is mandatory. The red beam ensures that you'll be able to maintain proper night vision while adjusting equipment and you won't ruin anyone else's shot.

Pack a few sealable plastic bags that are big enough to hold your equipment. Before you go back indoors after a night's shooting session put your camera gear in the sealed bag. This will help to prevent condensation building up inside your equipment.

Never breathe on the front element of your lens while you are out in the cold. Ice crystals will form on the glass and cause blurriness, ghosting and overall image degradation.

Infinity focus is of the utmost importance! In order to be 100% certain that your images are in focus you need to be sure that your lens is properly set to infinity. There are several ways to do this but I usually recommend that you use the digital zoom function while in live view mode to be sure that everything is perfect. Few things are more disappointing for an aurora photographer than to capture a once in a lifetime image only to discover that it is blurry!

Finally, before you book your trip research your destination thoroughly, because some locations offer far better chances of seeing lights than others due to local weather patterns. If you want to capture the perfect photograph of the aurora borealis, then book on to a reputable professional photographer's aurora borealis trip! The Arctic is an unforgiving location, and a guide's local knowledge can prove invaluable.

It is also important to make sure your guide has experience, so I highly recommend that you take a long look at their body of work. If the guide in question does not have an impressive portfolio of aurora images, it is likely that they will not be able to help you improve yours.

A HOTEL OF ICE

The Jukkasjärvi Ice Hotel, located in Swedish Lapland, was first constructed in 1990 as an igloo housing an art exhibition. The number of people involved in the innovative event meant that there was a shortage of accommodation available for them. Some of them were granted permission to sleep inside the ice structure in sleeping bags on top of reindeer skins: thus, the idea of an ice hotel was born.

Once the event was over, the idea evolved, and just two years later, in 1992, the public were permitted to stay in the specially created hotel suites, be married at the Ice Chapel, and drink at the Ice Bar.

Situated 200 km north of the Arctic Circle, the iconic Jukkasjärvi Ice Hotel is constructed anew each year, using snow and ice blocks. These are harvested during springtime from the river Torne, which is adjacent to the site. This is carefully stored until the hotel is built in the winter months, usually between November and December.

The snow, combined with ice to make 'snice', is used to form the structure of the hotel and the neighbouring ice chapel, while the blocks of ice are carved into elaborate designs for the suites and the ice bar inside. Everything

The Ice Hotel, Jukkasjärvi, Sweden. Photograph by Claire Edmonds.

within the hotel, from the glasses in the ice bar to the furniture in the art suites, is made from ice.

Each year ambitious designers will submit their ideas, and around fifty are selected to travel to Sweden and hand-carve their unique designs to be part of the now iconic attraction. This process guarantees that the ice hotel is different each year, while continuously showcasing new artists. The hotel is open from December until around April, when the rising temperatures start the melting process, returning the ice and snow to the river.

In addition to being the first hotel of this type, the Jukkasjärvi Ice Hotel is the largest. Covering up to 6,000 square meters, it is constructed from around 900 tonnes of ice and 21,500 tonnes of 'snice' each year. The hotel can accommodate up to 100 guests, in both ice rooms and warm cabins. In addition to those who stay overnight, there are also a large number of day visitors, meaning that the number of visitors totals at around 60,000 each year. Its extreme northern location also means that it provides an excellent opportunity for viewing the Northern Lights.

Top The Ice Hotel, Jukkasjärvi, Sweden.
Photograph by Claire Edmonds.

A team harvesting ice for next year's Ice Hotel,
Jukkasjärvi, Sweden. Photograph by Claire Edmonds.

The Ice Bar, inside the Ice Hotel, Jukkasjärvi, Sweden.
Designed by Torne River. Photograph by Claire Edmonds.

Furniture sculpted from ice, inside the Ice Hotel, Jukkasjärvi,
Sweden. Photograph by Claire Edmonds.

OFF THE MAP TRAVEL

It was while travelling back from a visit to Björkliden and Abisko that Jonny Cooper, the founder of *Off the Map Travel*, decided that he wanted to help give other people the opportunity to marvel at the stunning Northern Lights and experience the thrill of Arctic Sweden.

As a climbing, canoeing and mountain biking instructor Jonny had seen the growth of enthusiasm for adventure activities. At the same time he realised that a lot of people wanted to be adventurous without the 'soggy sandwich and cold cup of tea' which are so often associated with those types of holiday – and so *Off the Map Travel* was born.

Launching in 2010, Jonny brought together a passionate group of people, who themselves love adventure, to tailor-make trips specialising in a new niche of 'soft adventure'. People are given the opportunity to travel to stunning destinations such as Björkliden, which are both off the regular travel routes and which deliver adventure yet with a touch of comfort and even luxury.

Because each group, and each individual's interpretation of 'adventure', is different, it was important to Jonny and the team at *Off the Map Travel* that each trip is designed individually. This flexibility allows the team not only to create a trip that will leave lasting memories, but one which is organised to each person's exacting requirements and needs.

Often groups choose to visit locations whose natural environment is the principal attraction: it might be an amazing glacier in Greenland, forest habitats in western Sweden, or whale migration routes around Iceland. It is vital that the very act of visiting and enjoying such amazing destinations does not harm their environments. *Off the Map Travel* work hard to develop responsible travel policies to ensure that they preserve the very things that led the team to explore them in the first place

Climate change is also a pressing global issue facing us all, especially when considering international travel. Therefore, *Off the Map Travel* offset the carbon emissions from any flights associated with its trips, working closely with ClimateCare who reduce global greenhouse gas emissions on behalf of companies and individuals.

Today *Off the Map Travel* offer both summer and winter soft adventure holidays with a focus on different destinations that are easily accessible but not offered by many other tour operators. On the date of publication this includes Sweden, Norway, Finland, Iceland, Greenland, Gozo and the Spanish Pyrenees but they continue to expand as they find those destinations with something a little different.

It is, however, the stunning region of northern Sweden in Björkliden and Abikso that has always been so highly regarded by the team at *Off the Map Travel*, as it was here surrounded by snow and that arctic mountains, under the clear dark skies and thousands of stars that the Northern Lights appeared and inspired Jonny to help others to experience this incredible phenomenon.

www.offthemaptravel.co.uk

0800 566 8901

email: info@offthemaptravel.co.uk